HOPE

Devotional Prayers for The Hurting Heart

By David A. Edwards

To order additional copies of this book visit our website.

davidaedwardsonline.com

Copyright © 2009 by David A. Edwards. All rights reserved.

No part of this publication may be reproduced, stored in a retrieval system, or transmitted in any form or by any means – electronic, digital, photocopy, recording, or any other – except for brief quotations in printed reviews, without the prior written permission from David A. Edwards.

ISBN 1448651832

Unless otherwise indicated, all Scripture quotations are taken from the *Holy Bible,* New Living Translation, copyright © 1996. Used by permission of Tyndale House Publishers, Inc., Wheaton Illinois 60189. All right reserved.

Scripture quotations marked (NASB) are taken from the NEW AMERICAN STANDARD BIBLE®, Copyright 1960, 1962, 1963, 1968, 1971, 1972, 1973, 1975, 1977, 1995 by Lockman Foundation. Used by permission.

Scripture quotations marked (NIV) are taken from the HOLY BIBLE, NEW INTERNATIONAL VERSION®. Copyright © 1973, 1978, 1984 by International Bible Society. Used by permission of Zondervan Publishing House. All rights reserved.

The "NIV" and "New International Version" trademarks are registered in the United States Patent and Trademark Office by International Bible Society. Use of either trademark requires the permission of International Bible Society.

Dedication

For Those Who Hurt

May God give words to your heart through these prayers, and bring you the HOPE of His Eternal Love, Strength, and Care.

Oct 2016

Jenice,

I love you and am praying for you.

"I pick YOU!"

Love,

Dad

Table of Contents

Preface 9
Introduction 13
Daily Devotionals 17
-Day 1- Don't Despair 18
-Day 2- Close to the Brokenhearted 20
-Day 3- Forgiven 22
-Day 4- The Sting of Discipline 24
-Day 5- Dissolving Fears 26
-Day 6- Delight and Desires 28
-Day 7- Help 30
-Day 8- Heavenly Direction 32
-Day 9- Persistent Prayer 34
-Day 10- Strengthening 36
-Day 11- A Future and a Hope 38
-Day 12- Waiting 40
-Day 13- A Sovereign Tapestry 42
-Day 14- No Worries Mate 44
-Day 15- A Best Friend 46
-Day 16- Don't Hold Back 48
-Day 17- Stand Tall 50
-Day 18- His Care 52
-Day 19- Courageous Faith 54
-Day 20- Comfort and Strength 56
-Day 21- Restful Trust 58
-Day 22- Shelter in the Storm 60
-Day 23- A Purpose 62
-Day 24- Faith and Praise 64
-Day 25- Rest in Him 66
-Day 26- Soul Fitness 68
-Day 27- Bearing Burdens 70
-Day 28- Gratitude 72
-Day 29- His Peace 74
-Day 30- His Comfort 76
-Day 31- Faith and Obedience 78
-Day 32- Rest 80
-Day 33- His Understanding and Power 82
-Day 34- Renewal 84
-Day 35- A Lift 86
-Day 36- His Presence 88

- **Day 37-** His Provision 90
- **Day 38-** Friends 92
- **Day 39-** The Great Giver 94
- **Day 40-** Forgiveness and Obedience 96
- **Day 41-** Thy Word 98
- **Day 42-** Love Your Neighbor 100
- **Day 43-** A Generous Wisdom 102
- **Day 44-** Be Blessed 104
- **Day 45-** Pray Big 106
- **Day 46-** Your Mind and His Peace 108
- **Day 47-** A Cry for Mercy 110
- **Day 48-** Unfailing Love 112
- **Day 49-** Incomprehensible Love 114
- **Day 50-** Pour Out Your Troubles 116
- **Day 51-** A Sure Help 118
- **Day 52-** Get and Give Mercy 120
- **Day 53-** Draw Near 122
- **Day 54-** His Grace 124
- **Day 55-** As Unto the Lord 126
- **Day 56-** God our Father 128
- **Day 57-** The Wings of Eagles 130
- **Day 58-** The Great Healer 132
- **Day 59-** Calming the Storm 134
- **Day 60-** Bless the Children 136
- **Day 61-** Strength and Encouragement 138
- **Day 62-** Acts of Kindness 140
- **Day 63-** Living in Harmony 142
- **Day 64-** His Abundance 144
- **Day 65-** Live Close to Him 146
- **Day 66-** Embrace His Love 148
- **Day 67-** Feast Upon His Word 150
- **Day 68-** Rebuilding 152
- **Day 69-** Unfair Criticism 154
- **Day 70-** God's Protection from Enemies 156
- **Day 71-** Our Prayers, God's Miracles 158
- **Day 72-** Weeping ... then Joy 160
- **Day 73-** Compassion 162
- **Day 74-** Quiet Confidence 164
- **Day 75-** The Shepherd's Care 166
- **Day 76-** The Love of a Father 168
- **Day 77-** A Humble Heart 170
- **Day 78-** Nourishing the Soul 172

- **Day 79-** Calming the Emotional Storm 174
- **Day 80-** Groan Your Desires to God 176
- **Day 81-** Peaceable Wisdom 178
- **Day 82-** Love Him 180
- **Day 83-** The Promised Land 182
- **Day 84-** A Friend 184
- **Day 85-** Pour out the Pain 186
- **Day 86-** Hope Indeed 188
- **Day 87-** Life and Peace 190
- **Day 88-** A Restored Soul 192
- **Day 89-** Just Like Heaven 194
- **Day 90-** His Closeness 196

Preface

What follows in these pages is not a refined reflection of what lead me to a place of hope, but rather it is a raw record of a wounded heart during a time of unspeakable pain. The order of the devotionals is exactly as they flowed in my own healing process. It was consistent and honest time with my Heavenly Father, feeding on His word and expressing my heart to Him that God used to ultimately bring back my hope. My prayer is that somehow these glimpses into my heart will pull you down the same road of intimacy with God, and ultimately lead you to HOPE again.

Each devotional consists of a three parts:

SCRIPTURE

A passage(s) from the Bible is the basis for each prayer. Each written prayer has flowed from personal meditation of the Scripture passages quoted, and is based on the themes or principles found in the passage(s).

PRAYER

Each prayer was originally written as a prayer for myself during a deep time of loss, abandonment, and misunderstanding. Use these prayers as a tool in expressing to God something that may swirl around your own heart or experience, and pray truth into your own life.

ENCOURAGMENT

For each journal entry, I found it helpful to articulate an encouragement to myself, reinforcing some truth contained in the scripture. Use these as a way of cementing the truth into your heart. Go back to these encouragements often, and allow them to remind you, reorient you, and lift you above the circumstances of your pain.

NOTES

Journaling is a wonderfully rich part of the spiritual growth process. To that end, space has been provided for you to record some of your own thoughts and feelings as God touches your heart. Many have experienced journaling as a deep source of encouragement in the years that follow, as they look back and see the record of God's clear work at a tender time in their lives.

This book is intended to stimulate you to personal and daily time with God, both listening to Him from His word, and talking with Him through prayer. These devotionals are merely a starting place. May God draw you closer, and touch your heart deeply as you drink from the well of friendship with God Himself.

Introduction

Life is not always fair, and is sometimes filled with unspeakable pain. Aloneness, abandonment, fear, discouragement, anxiety, and emotional exhaustion are among the possible emotions I can feel, and are sometimes just a single event away in my life. My world changes in what seems like an instant, and I find myself in a world of suffering that I did not know existed, and seems untraveled by any other. I may be a victim, suffering because of tragedy or another's sin. I may be responsible for my own pain, suffering the consequence of my disobedience. Either way, the pain that I feel is very real and sometimes utterly overwhelming.

So how do I regain hope?

True and lasting hope can only be found in God Himself. If my hope is in my circumstance, and I suddenly discover that I cannot control my circumstance, then I will be without hope. If my hope is in my own perfection and righteousness, and I discover I am capable of sin, then hope will dissolve. If my hope is in any temporal things of this earth, I may find myself doomed to a life of hopelessness as those temporal things change without even asking me. But... if my hope is in a personal relationship with the Eternal, Sovereign and Forgiving God, then God can give me hope regardless of the circumstances of my temporal life. Pursuing personal relationship with my Lord is my only sure hope for this life, and the life to come, since that can never be taken away from me, no matter the circumstances.

There are at least two ingredients that God uses to create hope in our lives. Ironically, the first ingredient is the very circumstance that seems to steal hope. Listen to what Paul says about the relationship of difficult circumstances and hope:

> *And not only this, but we also exult in our tribulations, knowing that tribulation brings about perseverance; and perseverance, proven character; and proven character, hope; and hope does not disappoint..."*
>
> *(Romans 5:3-5 NASB)*

Tribulations can eventually lead to increased hope, if I am persevering and allowing God to refine my character in the process.

The second ingredient that leads to hope is the encouragement that comes from the Scriptures, the word of God.

> *For whatever was written in earlier times was written for our instruction, so that through perseverance and the encouragement of the Scriptures we might have hope.*
>
> *(Romans 15:4 NASB)*

As I go back to the Bible in a time of pain, I discover spiritual nourishment designed to create health of heart, mind and soul.

Very likely you have picked up, or been given this book because you are hurting and in need of hope. You may scoff at the thought that hope could ever be restored, given the depth of your pain. That's ok.

What follows are the Scriptures that touched my own heart at a time of deep pain, the prayers that flowed from my soul, and the encouragements from the Scriptures that lifted my heart.

May God do for you, what only HE can do...

> *"I pray that God, the source of hope, will fill you completely with joy and peace because you trust in him. Then you will overflow with confident hope through the power of the Holy Spirit."*
>
> *Romans 15:13*

Daily Devotionals

-Day 1-
Don't Despair

SCRIPTURE

"I would have despaired unless I had believed that I would see the goodness of the LORD in the land of the living. Wait for the LORD; be strong and let your heart take courage; yes, wait for the LORD."

Psalm 27:13-14

Now faith is the assurance of things hoped for...

Hebrews 11:1

PRAYER

Lord, I ask that you would breathe faith into my heart so that I know beyond a shadow of a doubt that one day I will enter the land and see the full measure of your goodness to me. Give me the assurance of those things I hope for. And between now and then, give me the strength and courage to wait for you LORD, yes to wait for you. Amen.

ENCOURAGEMENT

Believe. Be strong. Take courage. Wait. You can do this.

Notes

-Day 2-
Close to the Brokenhearted

SCRIPTURE

The eyes of the Lord watch over those who do right; his ears are open to their cries for help...
The Lord hears his people when they call to him for help. He rescues them from all their troubles.
The Lord is close to the brokenhearted; he rescues those whose spirits are crushed.
The righteous person faces many troubles, but the Lord comes to the rescue each time.
Psalm 34:16-19

PRAYER

Lord, I pray that you would encourage my heart to know that I am doing right, that your ears are hearing my cries for help, and that you are even now rescuing me from my troubles with a tapestry woven by your sovereign hand. I ask that you would double my portion of comforting angels, and brush me often with their wings so that I do not question your sweet presence. Touch my heart with your fullness, your comfort, your peace, your hope, your faith, and even a taste of your joy here and there... touch it deeply, and touch it often I pray. Amen.

ENCOURAGEMENT

Even this time He will come to the rescue... yes, even this time.

———————

Notes

-Day 3-
Forgiven

SCRIPTURE

For the choir director: A psalm of David, regarding the time Nathan the prophet came to him after David had committed adultery with Bathsheba.

Have mercy on me, O God, because of your unfailing love. Because of your great compassion, blot out the stain of my sins. Wash me clean from my guilt. Purify me from my sin. For I recognize my rebellion; it haunts me day and night. Against you, and you alone, have I sinned; I have done what is evil in your sight. You will be proved right in what you say, and your judgment against me is just...
Purify me from my sins, and I will be clean; wash me, and I will be whiter than snow. Oh, give me back my joy again; you have broken me—now let me rejoice. Don't keep looking at my sins. Remove the stain of my guilt. Create in me a clean heart, O God. Renew a loyal spirit within me. Do not banish me from your presence, and don't take your Holy Spirit from me. Restore to me the joy of your salvation, and make me willing to obey you. Then I will teach your ways to rebels, and they will return to you.... The sacrifice you desire is a broken spirit. You will not reject a broken and repentant heart, O God.

Psalm 51 (selected verses)

PRAYER

Lord, I ask that you would flood my heart with a profound sense of your complete forgiveness. I ask that you would help me to know that even this can be forgiven; that there is no sin that is so great that your powerful love cannot reach it, and your atonement cannot pay for it. Help me to feel the wash of your forgiveness deep within. Restore my confidence before you and before man. May I continue to move forward in ministry, knowing that you are pleased with a broken and repentant heart, and that your powerful Holy Spirit resides within me. And may the condemning eye of judgmental people pale in significance, as I see the brilliance of your forgiving and empowering love. Amen.

ENCOURAGEMENT

You are forgiven. Get up, brush yourself off, hold your head high, and move forward with the applause of Heaven.

Notes

-Day 4-
The Sting of Discipline

SCRIPTURE

5 And have you forgotten the encouraging words God spoke to you as his children? He said,
> "My child, don't make light of the Lord's discipline, and don't give up when he corrects you. 6 For the Lord disciplines those he loves, and he punishes each one he accepts as his child."

7 As you endure this divine discipline, remember that God is treating you as his own children. Who ever heard of a child who is never disciplined by its father? 8 If God doesn't discipline you as he does all of his children, it means that you are illegitimate and are not really his children at all. 9 Since we respected our earthly fathers who disciplined us, shouldn't we submit even more to the discipline of the Father of our spirits, and live forever? 10 For our earthly fathers disciplined us for a few years, doing the best they knew how. But God's discipline is always good for us, so that we might share in his holiness. 11 No discipline is enjoyable while it is happening—it's painful! But afterward there will be a peaceful harvest of right living for those who are trained in this way. 12 So take a new grip with your tired hands and strengthen your weak knees. 13 Mark out a straight path for your feet so that the limb which is lame will not be put out of joint further, but rather will be healed.

Hebrews 12:5-12

PRAYER

Lord, I have felt the heaviness of your discipline in recent days. You have been a loving and firm Father to me. You have shown the strong part of your love to me by using the sting of the consequences that flowed from my actions. Thank you for pressing that pain into my life, and for using that pain to produce the fruit of obedience. Because of my repentance, I ask that over the coming days you would pour a healing balm into my wounds. Refresh me. Give relief. Renew my perspective. Strengthen me. I pray that I would feel your smile as I walk a straight path, and that the memory of the pain of your discipline will keep me from wandering off that path. May I join that honorable band of sinners like King David, who repented, endured, healed, and went on to have an even more precise and powerful impact for you. Amen.

ENCOURAGEMENT

Don't give up. Stay close to the Shepherd of your soul. He has healing and hope on your horizon.

Notes

-Day 5-
Dissolving Fears

SCRIPTURE

"With his love, he will calm all your fears."
Zephaniah 3:16

PRAYER

Lord, I ask that you would make me feel the depth of your unfailing love at this very moment. May I know that your love is powerful, faithful, passionate, and pure. May I see that the fullness of your love is directed to me. Take all that I know and have felt of love, and use it to reveal to my heart the perfect beauty and strength of your love for me. Overwhelm me with your love. And as I feel the warmth of your love, I ask that you would melt away those fears... those fears about what the future holds... those fears about what others think... those fears about finance, friends, family, and fulfillment... those fears about aloneness and grief... those fears about anxiety and panic. Take them away Lord. As your passionate love swirls with your graciousness, dissolve those fears, each one, all at once, completely, and now. Give me this gift. Calm my fears with your love, I pray. Amen.

ENCOURAGEMENT

Fear not, for his love is unfailing. Rest in the strong arms of his love. Rest.

Notes

-Day 6-
Delight and Desires

SCRIPTURE

3 Trust in the Lord and do good.
Then you will live safely in the land and prosper.
4 Take delight in the Lord,
and he will give you your heart's desires.
Psalm 37:3-4

PRAYER

Lord, I ask that you would move my heart to embrace you as my most intimate delight. Make closeness to you the most important pursuit of my life. Be my best friend. Draw me to spend much quiet time sitting in your presence, listening to your words as they speak to my deep heart. Make me feel your presence in those moments, as if you were in the chair next to me. May that intimacy with you move me to trust you, to trust you so much that I do what is good, even when it is hard. And Lord, as I delight my soul in you, I ask that you would give me a cadence in my heart that you will indeed give me the desires of my heart. May I never resign myself to accepting less than my heart's desire. May I trust your goodness to me so profoundly that I know beyond a shadow of a doubt that you will fulfill my deepest longings. Never allow my hope to fade. And in those moments of deepest intimacy with you, may my heart's desires burn still with quiet intensity, and may a smile come to my soul as I imagine you, my loving heavenly Father, bestowing that gift from heaven. Give me those desires I pray. Give them soon. Amen.

ENCOURAGEMENT

Make our Lord the object of your most passionate delight, and watch what happens. He has not forgotten you. Believe.

Notes

-Day 7-
Help

SCRIPTURE

1 In times of trouble, may the Lord answer your cry.
May the name of the God of Jacob keep you safe from all harm.
2 May he send you help from his sanctuary
and strengthen you from Jerusalem.
3 May he remember all your gifts
and look favorably on your burnt offerings.
Interlude
4 May he grant your heart's desires
and make all your plans succeed.
5 May we shout for joy when we hear of your victory
and raise a victory banner in the name of our God.
May the Lord answer all your prayers.
Psalm 20:1-5

PRAYER

Lord, I have had some recent times of trouble, and have cried out to you in desperation. Please answer my cry. Please surround me with the safety that comes from a garrison of guardian angels, always protecting me from all harm. I ask that you would dispatch help by answering the specifics of my cry, and that you would supply a generous dose of supernatural strength to sustain me in the midst of trouble. Please be mindful of the sincerity of my worship and the genuineness of my sacrifice of obedience, and look favorably on both. Please Lord, give me the deepest desires of my heart, and make my plans successful. And I promise to give a joyous shout of praise to you as I feel my victory. Lord, I beg of you that you would see the clarity of my heart and answer each and every one of my prayers with an answer that is full, rich, and even overflowing. Amen.

ENCOURAGEMENT

God sees the genuineness of your heart, hears your cries for help, and will give you all that you need to face everything he allows. He will. Never stop crying out for his help. He loves your humble dependence.

Notes

-Day 8-
Heavenly Direction

SCRIPTURE

23 The Lord directs the steps of the godly. He delights in every detail of their lives. 24 Though they stumble, they will never fall, for the Lord holds them by the hand.

Psalm 37:23-24

PRAYER

What a great feeling Lord, to know that you actually delight in the details of my life. Wow. I pray that you would pervade my everyday with a constant picture of you, sitting at the edge of heaven, leaning forward with great interest. May I know that you love me so much that you relish every event, every nuance of emotion that glances across my heart, every mist of a thought that hovers at the edge of my mind. Make me know that your interest is active, speaking your voice into my heart as you ponder the small steps of my life, along with the giant leaps of change. And Lord, help me to feel your hand enveloping mine, as I walk, especially during those times when I stumble badly. May I feel your strength keeping me from falling headlong Lord. May I feel you righting my balance, and re-establishing my footing. And may I walk on with the confidence of walking hand in hand with my Heavenly Dad. Thank you, that although you are the Almighty God of the universe, you care deeply and daily for even me. Thank you indeed. Amen.

ENCOURAGEMENT

Relax. God will direct your steps, big and small. He will speak his still small voice, and you will hear. Just keep your hand in his, and you will be cared for and directed, even when you stumble profoundly.

Notes

-Day 9-
Persistent Prayer

SCRIPTURE

1   Then Jesus told his disciples a parable to show them that they should always pray and not give up.
2   He said: "In a certain town there was a judge who neither feared God nor cared about men.
3   And there was a widow in that town who kept coming to him with the plea, 'Grant me justice against my adversary.'
4   "For some time he refused. But finally he said to himself, 'Even though I don't fear God or care about men,
5   yet because this widow keeps bothering me, I will see that she gets justice, so that she won't eventually wear me out with her coming!'"
6   And the Lord said, "Listen to what the unjust judge says.
7   And will not God bring about justice for his chosen ones, who cry out to him day and night? Will he keep putting them off?
8   I tell you, he will see that they get justice, and quickly. However, when the Son of Man comes, will he find faith on the earth?"

Luke 18: 1-8 (NIV)

[Regarding Jesus in the Garden of Gethsemane just before his crucifixion]
35 He went on a little farther and fell to the ground. He prayed that, if it were possible, the awful hour awaiting him might pass him by. 36 "Abba, Father," he cried out, "everything is possible for you. Please take this cup of suffering away from me. Yet I want your will to be done, not mine."

Mark 14: 35-36

PRAYER

Lord, there is a quiet longing deep within my being, a desire of my heart. And yet, because of sin and circumstance I am tempted to give it up, to push it away, to stop believing, to pretend that I no longer long. But I cannot hide that passion from you; you see it and understand it completely, and I know that. I ask that you would place within me a renewed passion of persistence to "always pray and never give up." Fuel that in my heart. I ask that you would give me permission to, "plead with you day and night." I ask that you would give me permission to own the desires of my heart fully, and pray them unashamedly, just as you prayed yours in the Garden, and yet fully submit my will to yours. May I give up the scheme, but never the dream. May I leave the "how" to your sovereign power, but never give up the "what" of my deepest longings. Fortify my faith, so that I believe with every ounce of my soul that you WILL indeed answer my prayer, and "quickly". May I be one of the few whom you find to have faith when you return. And when my faith is weak, remind me that I am not alone, that there are others who join me in my prayers with enough faith to make up for my occasional lack. Lord, as I plead with you, I ask that you would release within me a wellspring of fresh hope.
Amen.

ENCOURAGEMENT

Own your longings. Plead them continually. Submit your will to his. But, never, never, never, ever give up.

Notes

-Day 10-
Strengthening

SCRIPTURE

The eyes of the Lord search the whole earth in order to strengthen those whose hearts are fully committed to him.

2 Chronicles 16:9

PRAYER

Lord, secure my unreserved commitment to you. Melt my discouragement. Fortify my faith. I ask that you would make my heart love you more than anything or anyone on the face of this earth. I pray that I would leap within at the thought of your love, at the sound of your word to me, at the look of your creation. I pray that the embrace of your grace would be better than skin. Make your presence such a reality to my everyday that I could not imagine living life without you. I pray that my heart would feel a passion of commitment to you that surpasses even the beauty of marital love. And as a result of this fully committed heart, I ask that in your search you would find me, lavish your pleasure on me, and powerfully strengthen me... today... now... at this very moment. And I ask that you would give me a special gift today... a gift that assures me of your presence and strengthening power... something unexpected... something profound. Please do that for me today. In faith, Amen.

ENCOURAGEMENT

Know that as God's eyes searched the earth, the brilliant quality of your heart caught his attention, and he paused to strengthen you. And his strength means something... something powerful and profound. Feel honored, and supported.

Notes

-Day 11-
A Future and a Hope

SCRIPTURE

O Lord my God, you have performed many wonders for us. Your plans for us are too numerous to list. You have no equal. If I tried to recite all your wonderful deeds, I would never come to the end of them.
Psalm 40:5

For I know the plans I have for you," says the Lord. "They are plans for good and not for disaster, to give you a future and a hope.
Jeremiah 29:11

PRAYER

Lord, great is thy faithfulness to me; great indeed. I ask that in this moment you would flood my heart with memory upon memory of your goodness to me. Remind me of the miracles, great and small, that you have done for me. Bring back to my heart the details of each, and the feelings that flowed as I experienced you, first hand. As I lay upon my bed, recalling your wonderful deeds, may I fall asleep before my list ends... and may this worship of gratitude assure my deep heart again that your plans for my future are also too numerous to list. Miracles will continue. Wonders will abound. Good will come. May the worship of my slumber be a sweet fragrance to you Lord. Amen.

ENCOURAGEMENT

God's past faithfulness is proof... his present gifts affirm it... he has plans for you that are good. He will give you a future. Today's buds of hope will become tomorrow's blossoms of goodness. Savor the buds today.

Notes

-Day 12-
Waiting

SCRIPTURE

Be still in the presence of the Lord, and wait patiently for him to act.

Psalm 37:7

PRAYER

Oh Lord, why do I find myself waiting again? How long, oh Lord, how long? When will you act? Does the waiting ever stop? These are the questions that simmer in my heart Lord. I long for an answer. Sometimes even "no" seems better than "wait". I ask that just now, you would give rest to my deepest place, Oh Lord. Just as you calmed the storm, speak stillness to the anxious waves of my heart. Reach out, and put your hand on mine. Look into my eyes and tell me that it will be ok. Pull me close, and hold me in your strong, calming arms. Rock my heart gently until it stills. Relax my mind, and give it the rest that only you can give. And as your closeness overwhelms me, and stillness presides, I ask that patient faith would emerge. Lord, I pray that waiting would become an anticipation of faith rather than a drudgery of longsuffering. I ask that the assurance of your coming action would transform waiting from restless to restful. May I be so consumed by your presence, that the moments of waiting actually seem sweet to my soul. And Lord, I pray with all my heart that one day I will see you clearly act, and the waiting will be over. Amen and Amen.

ENCOURAGEMENT

When you enter the Promised Land, it will be worth the wait. That's a promise.

Notes

-Day 13-
A Sovereign Tapestry

SCRIPTURE

And we know that God causes everything to work together for the good of those who love God and are called according to his purpose for them.
                                    Romans 8:28

PRAYER

Lord, some of my life has simply been a storm of raw pain and numbing loss. There is no explanation except the simple reality that sin and death are part of life. Some of this has come as if by chance, some by consequence; some by other's actions, some by mine. Some seems unjust, and some deserved. Much heartache has accrued, and much substance has been lost. And in my weak moments I feel as if nothing good can come of such loss, that the damage is unsalvageable, the circumstance unredeemable. Oh God in heaven above, make me to know the raw power of your sovereignty to weave from the threads of sin and death, a glorious tapestry of beauty and grace. Just as David and Bathsheba's sinful beginnings ultimately gave birth to the great Solomon, and eventually Messiah, and just as Esther became queen through a circumstance of sin and you used her to save a nation, I ask that you would assure me that my current pain is only a thread in the great tapestry of my life. And I ask Lord, that you would be weaving even now. I pray that you would use the dark backdrop of failure to enhance the brilliant diamonds of your powerful grace. I pray that you would twist that which seems hopeless into a weave of joy. I pray that the months to come would leave me agape with amazement as I relish the unveiling of that which I would never have even dared to dream. Surprise and delight me with your sovereign grace Lord. And in this moment, I ask that you would give me enough faith to ready myself today for the celebration tomorrow. Amen.

ENCOURAGEMENT

God is working, even now. He is weaving masterfully, secretly. Have faith. Have faith.

Notes

-Day 14-
No Worries Mate

SCRIPTURE

Don't worry about anything; instead, pray about everything. Tell God what you need, and thank him for all he has done. Then you will experience God's peace, which exceeds anything we can understand. His peace will guard your hearts and minds as you live in Christ Jesus.

Philippians 4:6-7

PRAYER

Lord, you know that at times my mind swirls with things over which I have no control; the future, other's thoughts, past events. And as my mind churns, my heart becomes anxious with worry, consternating over things for which I am not responsible; things that I can never change. Lord, I ask that you would draw my heart into that peaceful place of prayer. I pray that I would be moved to take each and every individual worry, and come to you with a very specific request. May I ask you to prevent that which I worry might be, to make true that which I worry might never be. Permeate my prayers with gratitude for the goodness you lavished upon me, and so fortify my prayers with faith in your continued graciousness. And if anxiety presses, may my prayers press more. May I linger in this place until anxiety dissolves into peace. Lord, take away every ripple of my heart, and make me as calm as a mountain lake on a still morning. Amaze me with your peace, Lord, and by it guard my mind from the chaotic swirl, and my heart from the burdensome weight. Garrison me about with a legion of calming angels, assuring me of your fatherly care. And may I hear once again your voice whispering in my ear, "I

love you, I love you, I love you, I love you, I love you."
Amen

ENCOURAGEMENT

Remember, one day your heart WILL say, "Today is turning out to be much better than tomorrow was going to be yesterday." One day. One day.

Notes

-Day 15-
A Best Friend

SCRIPTURE

O Lord, you have examined my heart and know everything about me. You know when I sit down or stand up. You know my thoughts even when I'm far away. You see me when I travel and when I rest at home. You know everything I do. You know what I am going to say even before I say it, Lord. You go before me and follow me. You place your hand of blessing on my head. Such knowledge is too wonderful for me, too great for me to understand!

Psalm 139:1-6

PRAYER

Lord, I feel so misunderstood, so unheard. My deep heart aches for a best friend, someone who cares, someone who longs to hear what lies beneath, someone who will listen long enough to hear, someone who will stand in my skin and understand. There is none. The ones I look to are either unwilling, or unable. I feel desperate and utterly alone. To whom can I turn? I turn to you, Lord. You made me. You know everything about me. You examine me completely, and know my deep heart even better than I. You understand what others misunderstand. You look beyond my actions, and see my heart. You not only listen to my words and understand, but you know them before I even speak them. Lord, there is nothing in my heart that is a mystery to you. You see me as I am, good and bad. And this deep heart understanding is overwhelming to me. Suddenly I feel heard. I feel understood by the one who matters. Thank you for making me important, for never pushing me aside, for always listening, for completely understanding. Thank you. I need you, especially in this season, on this day, and in this moment. Hold my heart in your caring hands, I pray. Amen.

ENCOURAGEMENT

God always listens. He knows. He understands. He cares. Cling to him. He will never let you down. Never.

———————————

Notes

-Day 16-
Don't Hold Back

SCRIPTURE

1 I cry out to God; without holding back. Oh, that God would listen to me!
2 When I was in deep trouble, I searched for the Lord. All night long I prayed, with hands lifted toward heaven, pleading. There can be no joy for me until he acts.
3 I think of God, and I moan, overwhelmed with longing for his help.

Psalm 77: 1-3

PRAYER

Lord, thank you that you can handle the full flow of my deepest emotions. With respect, and yet with full honestly, move me to articulate to you all that I feel. Lord, I ask that I would bring before you the deepest trouble of my soul, and pray it out to you. I ask that I would turn those sleepless nights into nights of honest pleading with hands lifted toward heaven. May I not run from my desire for you to act, but plead it aloud on my pillow. Lord, give me permission to feel, to moan with longing for your help. May I not hold back. And Lord, I ask that I would feel your smile as you see behind my pleas, that quiet resolve not to take things into my own hands. I pray that you would honor that by attending to the cry of my deep heart, and acting. And may my pleading melt into a slumber of peaceful faith. Amen.

ENCOURAGEMENT

Don't run from your heart. Tell him what you long for. Give him the details. Long. Plead. Build your case. He can handle it... and he is listening.

———————

Notes

-Day 17-
Stand Tall

SCRIPTURE

[Paul, questioning his own faithfulness to God]
"What about me, have I been faithful? Well, it matters very little what you or anyone else thinks. I don't even trust my own judgment on this point. My conscience is clear, but that isn't what matters. It is the Lord himself who will examine me and decide. So be careful not to jump to conclusions before the Lord returns as to whether or not someone is faithful."

1 Corinthians 4: 1-4

PRAYER

O Lord, you are the one who will examine me when you return. You will look past the confusion, and see my deep places. You will see the shortcomings, but you will also see the humility, the remorse, and the repentance. And even today, it is only what you think that matters. Press that reality into my heart. As I feel the judgment of others pressing in on me, either real or perceived, make it matter not. Make my humble state and your forgiveness blend together to form my confidence. I am forgiven, whatever others may think. Cause me to stand tall in your grace. It is your favor that rests on me today, affirming my straight path of obedience. Make the mist of human accusations evaporate in the sunshine of your grace. Make me to know, in my quiet moments, that you are pleased with me. I ask that your pleasure would so far out-weigh the opinions of people, that I would walk the streets as though walking with the Almighty himself. Make me know deeply the affirmation of your love and the peace of your pleasure. And may it shape my view of self both in this moment and forever... a sinner forgiven by your grace... a sheep secure in your care... an instrument ready to be used in your hand. Amen.

ENCOURAGEMENT

Stand tall in the sunshine of our Lord's forgiveness and favor. His opinion is what matters... and only his opinion. Your heart before him is right, and that is what is real, no matter what anyone else says or thinks. Period. S T A N D T A L L.

Notes

-Day 18-
His Care

SCRIPTURE

You keep track of all my sorrows.
   You have collected all my tears in your bottle.
   You have recorded each one in your book.
Psalm 56:8

What is the price of two sparrows—one copper coin? But not a single sparrow can fall to the ground without your Father knowing it. And the very hairs on your head are all numbered. So don't be afraid; you are more valuable to God than a whole flock of sparrows.
Matthew 10:29-31

Look at the lilies of the field and how they grow. They don't work or make their clothing, yet Solomon in all his glory was not dressed as beautifully as they are. And if God cares so wonderfully for wildflowers that are here today and thrown into the fire tomorrow, he will certainly care for you. Why do you have so little faith?
Matthew 6:28b-30

PRAYER

Lord, thank you that you care so deeply for me. Help my faith. I ask that as I feel the pain of sorrow in my heart, you would remind me that your attention and concern run so deep that you have bottled every tear, whether shed or not. You remember. I pray that as I see a stray hair on my pillow, that I would feel your attentive care revise the count of the hairs on my head in that instant. I ask that as I awake in the morning to the sweet music of the birds, that I would be reminded of my worth to you as the day begins. And I ask that the next time I ponder the beauty of a flower, and marvel at your attention to the intricate detail of each variety, that I would be impressed with your care of them. And then, as I watch the beauty of those flowers slowly wither...that I would know in that moment your surpassing care for ME. Lord, take these simple pictures, and use them to mark me with a true awareness of your constant, sustaining, enduring love and care for me. Amen.

ENCOURAGEMENT

As the flowers fade, know that his attentive care for you will not. You are supremely important to him. It is you he loves. You.

Notes

-Day 19-
Courageous Faith

SCRIPTURES

Moses gave the men these instructions as he sent them [the spies] out to explore the land: "Go north through the Negev into the hill country. See what the land is like...

After exploring the land for forty days, the men returned to Moses, Aaron...This was their report to Moses: "We entered the land you sent us to explore, and it is indeed a bountiful country—a land flowing with milk and honey... But the people living there are powerful, and their towns are large and fortified. We even saw giants there, the descendants of Anak! The Amalekites live in the Negev, and the Hittites, Jebusites, and Amorites live in the hill country. The Canaanites live along the coast of the Mediterranean Sea and along the Jordan Valley... We can't go up against them! They are stronger than we are!"...

Then Moses and Aaron fell face down on the ground before the whole community of Israel. Two of the men who had explored the land, Joshua son of Nun and Caleb son of Jephunneh, tore their clothing. They said to all the people of Israel, "The land we traveled through and explored is a wonderful land! And if the Lord is pleased with us, he will bring us safely into that land and give it to us. It is a rich land flowing with milk and honey. Do not rebel against the Lord, and don't be afraid of the people of the land. They are only helpless prey to us! They have no protection, but the Lord is with us! Don't be afraid of them!"

Numbers 13-14 (selected scriptures)

PRAYER

Lord, your faithfulness to give me the desires of my heart will one day bring me to the brink of the Promised Land. And you will require of me a courageous faith to enter. As I stand, gazing at this land flowing with milk and honey I will no doubt see the giants... the obstacles that appear to be impossible to ever overcome. Most around me will affirm that the giants are simply too tall and too strong and too many. "It will never work," they will say. And they will lure me to the safe mediocrity of another 40 years in the desert. I ask you today that you would fortify my faith in preparation for that moment of decision. Assure me now that you are pleased with me, that you are present with me, and that your power can bring me safely into the land no matter how overwhelming the obstacles may seem. Shrink the giants, Lord. Enlarge my confidence in your wisdom and power. Ready me today for the battle tomorrow. And may I rest with a peaceful trust in you. Amen.

ENCOURAGEMENT

Wait with the anticipation of faith for that moment. And then follow our Lord's touch of your heart rather than the multitude. Swallow your fear, gird your sword and follow your Lord into battle. He will not let you down. And the honey will indeed be sweet and plentiful.

Notes

-Day 20-
Comfort and Strength

SCRIPTURE

Now may our Lord Jesus Christ Himself and God our Father, who has loved us and given us eternal comfort and good hope by grace, comfort and strengthen your hearts in every good work and word.

II Thessalonians 2:16-17

PRAYER

Lord, you are indeed the one who has loved me. Make my heart feel the passion and depth of that love. You are indeed the one who has comforted me. Spread the warmth and calm of that comfort over me just now. You are indeed the one who has given me hope. May I awaken with a sense that all will be well, no matter how difficult it may seem. You are indeed the one who has given me grace. Wash me anew with your undeserved forgiveness and favor. And Lord, you are the one who gives strength to my heart. Please use the works of my day, and the words that land on my soul as a means to infuse raw strength into my heart, a strength that can endure the sting of the storms, the persistence of the pelting rain, and the bitterness of the biting winds. May comfort and strength reside side-by-side in my heart and provide that wonderful blend of calm, dignified endurance. Amen.

ENCOURAGEMENT

The love you desire, the comfort you relish, the hope you long for, and the strength you must have... all come from our Lord himself. Open your heart and receive them. He will lavish them with generosity.

Notes

-Day 21-
Restful Trust

SCRIPTURE

Trust in the Lord with all your heart
And do not lean on your own understanding.
Seek his will in all you do
And he will direct your paths.

Proverbs 3:5-6

PRAYER

Lord, I admit to you that sometimes I just don't understand the "ways" and "whys" of your work in my life. I cannot escape the impact that people and events have on my heart, sometimes a profoundly life-changing impact, and sometimes flowing from sin and death. It just does not seem right or fair Lord. I long to make sense of the pieces, and see the puzzle of my life through your eyes. The master plan is a mystery to me. I wish that I could know the end. My mind stews, trying to sort and collate and synthesize events and responses into some order, to see what glue of truth might hold it all together. I want to know, to understand, so that I can somehow rest on that understanding. But alas, it is the leaning on my own understanding that is the opposite of trust in you. So I stop. I pause. I take rest from my frenzy of calculation and lean myself on you Lord. I allow myself to freefall into your arms, releasing my need to understand and resting my whole heart in your capable and loving fatherliness. I am content to see through the fog of my life, just the next few steps of the road, and to walk that path in faith. I know that you see the end, in fact you have already woven the whole of my life into a purposeful design. I want what you want Lord. I acknowledge you and seek your will in every step. And as I do, I thank you for the confidence of your faithful direction. I promise that I will pause long at every crossroad in my life, and seek your direction. I promise to follow you, even when it seems not to fit the mold. Your will is my only hope. You have my heart. Amen.

ENCOURAGEMENT

Reach down into the deepest place of your heart, and allow yourself to sink into a restful trust in him. Don't be consumed with calculating the end. Just walk the path. Walk it a step at a time. And be ready for the day the fog lifts, and the milk and honey begin to flow. Be ready.

Notes

-Day 22-
Shelter in the Storm

SCRIPTURE

Have mercy on me, O God, have mercy.
For my soul looks to you for protection;
I will hide beneath the shadow of your wings until the violent storm passes by.
Psalm 57:1

PRAYER

Mercy indeed, is what I need O God. I am lost without your strong protection in these times of violence to my soul. I ask that you would stoop down to this undeserving one, and show kindness to me this day. I know that there is no other place that I can go to find shelter from this storm, no other place that is secure enough to offer true protection from the potential devastation. And I know that I do not deserve this grace... that is why it is called mercy. Have mercy, O God. It is my soul that looks for your protection, for refuge, for a hiding place. The ravages of self and sin, the condemning eyes of my enemies, the silence of those who were my brothers, the open wounds of the years that continue to be lanced; these are some elements of the storm that buffet my soul still. And yet, I have found a hiding place in the shadow of your wing, O Lord. As I climb underneath your strong care, it is as if the door is closed to the storm. The sound of the rain is more distant; the sting of the wind is rebuffed; the warmth of your closeness replaces the bite of the cold. Your strong arm pulls me closer still as your mercy envelops me. And here I stay, waiting, longing, trusting, until the violence subsides, and you release me to again enjoy the warmth of the sunshine. Thank you Lord, for shelter, for mercy... and for the storm that has pressed me to you. I promise never again to take the sunshine for granted, never again to rest in my own sufficiency, and always to remember the mercy you have shown today. I promise to thank you tomorrow, with the same tear-filled fervency of my pleadings today. In fact, I pause now... and thank you today for the sunshine yet to come. Amen.

ENCOURAGEMENT

Run to him. He will open his wings and receive you. He will shelter your soul. And when the storm is passed, and the sunshine emerges, life will be greener from the rain, and clearer from the wind. Remember, the sun is shining even now, behind the clouds. Watch for the silver lining. Watch what God will do.

Notes

-Day 23-
A Purpose

SCRIPTURE

I cry out to God Most High, to God who will fulfill his purpose for me. He will send help from heaven to rescue me, disgracing those who hound me. My God will send forth his unfailing love and faithfulness.
                                                    Psalm 57:2-3

PRAYER

Lord, lift my heart this day with the reassurance that you have a purpose for me; a high purpose; a purpose that will honor you and impact others with my quality and giftedness. I know that as I sit alone in the midst of the storm, doubt assails me. I wonder if I have missed your purpose. I muse that somehow my failure has thwarted your plan. I fear that the gifts you have given me will go to waste. Ah but Lord, YOU are the one who will fulfill my purpose, by your rescuing help, from the depth of your unfailing love and faithfulness, and in response to my cry to you. Hear my cry Lord. May my cry be specific, persistent, and bold. May I ask you for great things, not great in the eyes of man, but great in the quiet place where only you see. Lord, fill me with a passion for faithfulness to you, faithfulness to use my gifts to your honor. And may I know that I can do that, even when no one but you is listening. It is your heart that is lifted as I make the music of my gifts, as the songs of my soul come out through those gifts. Lord, make me sing that song; make me sing it to you. And reward me in the deep place of my soul as I honor you in the quiet place of my life. Give me the faith to know that one day you will make the quality of my song an instrument of healing and grace to many. YOU will do that Lord. Help my faith. Give me hope.

Lift my heart today, please I pray. Refresh me by the gifts you have given me. Amen.

ENCOURAGEMENT

He has gifted you. He has a purpose for you. Today he is shaping, sanding, polishing, and tuning you. And one day he will present you as a well-tuned instrument, with the song of your soul touching many. One day.

Notes

-Day 24-
Faith and Praise

SCRIPTURE

7 My heart is confident in you, O God;
   my heart is confident.
   No wonder I can sing your praises!
8 Wake up, my heart!
   Wake up, O lyre and harp!
   I will wake the dawn with my song.
9 I will thank you, Lord, among all the people.
   I will sing your praises among the nations.
10 For your unfailing love is as high as the heavens.
   Your faithfulness reaches to the clouds.
Psalm 57:7-10

PRAYER

Lord, I pray confidence into my heart right now; confidence in you Lord. I pray that I would so trust in your unfailing love and faithfulness, that I would know beyond a doubt that you will answer me. Lord, please help my faith. I ask that you would take those pictures in this passage, and put them before me as reminders of who you are. As I slumber, and am vaguely aware of day breaking, I ask that you would put a simple song of praise in my heart. As I hear the wind instruments, and sees the elegance of the harp, may my heart be lifted in praise to you. As I look out at the full moon, and the clouds above the sunset, may I be reminded of the height of your unfailing love, and the reach of your faithfulness. And Lord, make all of this fortify the confidence I have in you. May I trust, may I rest, may I glory in you. And as I do, may hope spring forth... and shine on all I do. May I wake the dawn with my song tomorrow, because of my confidence in you today. Amen.

ENCOURAGEMENT

Look long upon the full moon. Be still and gaze upon the clouds. Allow your heart to play the harp strings of praise. Remember... he loves you... he will be faithful to you... he is worthy of your song of praise. Sing it today in anticipation of what he will give tomorrow. Raise your voice to him.

Notes

-Day 25-
Rest in Him

SCRIPTURE

[Jesus said] "Come to Me, all who are weary and heavy-laden, and I will give you rest. Take My yoke upon you and learn from Me, for I am gentle and humble in heart, and YOU WILL FIND REST FOR YOUR SOULS. For My yoke is easy and My burden is light."

Matthew 11:28-30

PRAYER

Rest for my soul Lord, I pray rest for my soul. I come to you in my weariness, and the excessive load of the burden I carry. I come and rest. Make my heart cease from its churning. Make my mind stop trying to calculate the sum of the parts of my life and circumstances. Gently stop me Lord, and quiet me. May I lay down this night, sinking into your arms, and rest in you. And as I rise, may I simply continue obeying you, taking your yoke, doing what is right today, leaving tomorrow for you to care for. I pray that as I obey, that your smile would shine upon my soul, and that the weariness would melt away. Rest Lord, rest is what I pray into my life this day. Amen.

ENCOURAGEMENT

Take a deep breath, and let out a big sigh... and rest in him. You have come already. You have taken his yoke, and are doing what is right. Now rest. Rest. You are in his care.

Notes

-Day 26-
Soul Fitness

SCRIPTURE

Dear brothers and sisters, when troubles come your way, consider it an opportunity for great joy. For you know that when your faith is tested, your endurance has a chance to grow. So let it grow, for when your endurance is fully developed, you will be perfect and complete, needing nothing. If you need wisdom, ask our generous God, and he will give it to you. He will not resent your asking.

James 1:2-5

PRAYER

Lord, I admit to you that I really don't like it when troubles come my way. It hurts, it's confusing, and I seem to either feel guilt or injustice, depending on the cause of the trouble. I sometimes feel like I am pressing the barbell up, up, up, squeezing out that last repetition of the third set while my shoulders scream out with that clear burn of muscle fatigue. It hurts. But then I realize, Lord, that the pain is not destructive to my life, but is producing an increase in the strength and endurance in my character that will make me more spiritually fit for worship and ministry. And at that moment of realization, the pain actually feels different, Lord, it feels healthy. When I think back on the accumulation of strength and endurance that has accrued over the years, I begin to feel something under the pain, something deeper and more profound. I begin to feel joy; a sense of fulfillment as I taste the fruit of increased personal soul-fitness. Lord, keep my perspective clear. Keep my heart longing for growth. And make me willing to walk the road of fatigue to get this growth. Give me more moments of joy along the way, I ask. Amen.

ENCOURAGEMENT

Keep walking the treadmill of God's path before you. Even when you don't feel you are making any progress, your soul-fitness is increasing bit by bit, and the muscles of your faith are tightening. And it will pay off. So keep walking, and allow yourself to feel the joy of growth.

———————————

Notes

-Day 27-
Bearing Burdens

SCRIPTURE

29   But he wanted to justify himself, so he asked Jesus, "And who is my neighbor?"
30   In reply Jesus said: "A man was going down from Jerusalem to Jericho, when he fell into the hands of robbers. They stripped him of his clothes, beat him and went away, leaving him half dead.
31   A priest happened to be going down the same road, and when he saw the man, he passed by on the other side.
32   So too, a Levite, when he came to the place and saw him, passed by on the other side.
33   But a Samaritan, as he traveled, came where the man was; and when he saw him, he took pity on him.
34   He went to him and bandaged his wounds, pouring on oil and wine. Then he put the man on his own donkey, took him to an inn and took care of him.
35   The next day he took out two silver coins and gave them to the innkeeper. 'Look after him,' he said, 'and when I return, I will reimburse you for any extra expense you may have.'
36   "Which of these three do you think was a neighbor to the man who fell into the hands of robbers?"
37   The expert in the law replied, "The one who had mercy on him." Jesus told him, "Go and do likewise."
Luke 10:33-37 (NIV)

"Do not judge so that you will not be judged."
Matthew 7:1

"Carry each other's burdens, and in this way you will fulfill the law of Christ." (Galatians 6:2)

PRAYER

Lord, I seek to be a person with a caring heart, to truly understand love. I desire to listen deeply to the true heart, and not to judge on past actions alone. In fact, I strive not to judge at all, but just to reach out with humility and forgiveness. I know that even the heart that has wandered hurts. Keep me from asking where the wounds came from, and judging the worthiness of the wounded. May I simply see the wounds, refuse to pass by on the other side of the road, and reach out to give what I can toward healing. Move me to call, to write, to show hospitality, to encourage, to pray, and to even talk straight when the time is right. Make me a friend. Make me a true neighbor. May I give my strength to help shoulder a load that is too heavy to carry alone. Lord, I ask that at this very moment you would smile upon me. Give me a taste today of the reward of loving others with your love. May I know that you are making a difference through me. And may I be encouraged. Amen.

ENCOURAGEMENT

Your forgiving and gracious touch to others has been profound. Rest in your eternal reward.

Notes

-Day 28-
Gratitude

SCRIPTURE

We thank you, O God! We give thanks because you are near. People everywhere tell of your wonderful deeds.
Psalm 75:1

PRAYER

Lord, I pray that you would nurture my soul with gratitude today. As my will identifies and expresses gratitude for your wonderful deeds, I ask that you would feed the emotion of gratefulness within. May my list be long Lord, and when I begin to come to the end I ask that you would stretch my heart to look even more deeply at who you are, and what that means in my life. Lord, again I pray that you would open my eyes to see just how near you are to me, how present you are in my everyday, how close you were today. Make me feel your nearness, like a good friend. May I feel the warmth of your presence in the sunshine, and the comfort of your presence in my sleep. Surprise and amaze me today with your nearness, Lord. Amen.

ENCOURAGEMENT

Count your blessings. Recall some of his wonderful deeds to you. Name them to him, everyday at least once. And watch your awareness of his nearness grow.

Notes

-Day 29-
His Peace

SCRIPTURE

You will keep in perfect peace
  all who trust in you,
  all whose thoughts are fixed on you!

Isaiah 26:3

PRAYER

Lord, today I ask that you would calm the storm... the storm within me. I pray that you would lay your hand upon my heart, and command the waves of anxiety to cease from churning. Lay the stillness of peace within me, Lord. Please take away the storm clouds on the horizon of today that threaten tomorrow. Make the wind of your comfort simply blow them away. And shine around them the silver lining of your grace. I pray that you would move me to fix my thoughts on you, Lord. May I remember the real touch of your comforting angels, your strengthening hand, your sustaining grace, your provisions and your care. May I be so calmed with the memory of your goodness that I can not but trust you for tomorrow. May my mind be so filled up with you that a flood of peace overtakes my worries and drowns them all. And Lord, when you give me that peace, please make it a perfect peace. Please. Amen.

ENCOURAGEMENT

Take control of your mind, and fix it on the memory of the good things God has given you. Dwell on his goodness and grace. Saturate yourself with thoughts of our Lord. And trust that his peace will follow.

Notes

-Day 30-
His Comfort

SCRIPTURE

Blessed be the God and Father of our Lord Jesus Christ, the Father of mercies and God of all comfort, who comforts us in all our affliction so that we will be able to comfort those who are in any affliction with the comfort with which we ourselves are comforted by God.

2 Corinthians 1:3-4

"Blessed are those who mourn, for they shall be comforted.

Matthew 5:4

PRAYER

Lord, today I ask that you would send an angelic messenger to me, carrying a double measure of your comfort to be poured directly into my heart. And after that another, and another, and then another, until I am filled up and overflowing. You know that I need that comfort today, this morning, this moment. So please give it generously. Push out the sense of loss, and replace it with the memories that have been gifted to me over the years. I pray that I would be truly blessed as your comfort washes over my mourning. And Lord, as I linger in that place of peaceful comfort, I ask that you would bring me a new gift, a gift of hope. I pray that I would know beyond a doubt that you see the true dream of my deep heart, and that you are promising to fulfill the desire of my heart as I delight in you. I ask that I would see the serendipitous events of yesterday as evidence of your sovereign tapestry, and so would be moved to trust you for tomorrow... giving me hope for today. And just as I begin to feel this new hope begin to rise on the horizon of my future, send another brigade of angels with triple loads of comfort. Overwhelm me with your love today. Amen.

ENCOURAGEMENT

He knows. He cares. He understands. And he is there for you, pouring out his comfort. You have felt it before, feel it again today. Receive his blessing.

Notes

-Day 31-
Faith and Obedience

SCRIPTURE

Now it came about after these things, that God tested Abraham, and said to him, "Abraham!" ...Take now your son, your only son, whom you love, Isaac, and go to the land of Moriah, and offer him there as a burnt offering on one of the mountains of which I will tell you." So Abraham rose early in the morning and saddled his donkey, and took two of his young men with him and Isaac his son; and he split wood for the burnt offering, and arose and went to the place of which God had told him.... Then they came to the place of which God had told him; and Abraham built the altar there and arranged the wood, and bound his son Isaac and laid him on the altar, on top of the wood. Abraham stretched out his hand and took the knife to slay his son. But the angel of the LORD called to him from heaven and said, "Abraham, Abraham!" And he said, "Here I am." He said, "Do not stretch out your hand against the lad, and do nothing to him; for now I know that you fear God, since you have not withheld your son, your only son, from Me."
Genesis 22:1-12 (selected NASB)

By faith Abraham, when he was tested, offered up Isaac, and he who had received the promises was offering up his only begotten son; it was he to whom it was said, "IN ISAAC YOUR DESCENDANTS SHALL BE CALLED." He considered that God is able to raise people even from the dead...
Hebrews 11:17-19 (NASB)

"For whoever wishes to save his life will lose it; but whoever loses his life for My sake will find it.
Matthew 16:25 (NASB)

PRAYER

Lord, I admit the agony of obeying you when it means giving up the gifts most precious to me. The pain of release is unspeakable. And yet, I do it. I release my hold. I choose obedience because of faith. But Lord, I hear the flesh of my heart tearing as roots of self are being extracted. I truly feel that I am loosing my life for the sake of obedience to you. And then I remember the faith of Abraham, who trusted you so much that he believed you could give him the promise even if you had to raise Isaac from the dead. Lord, please give me a faith like that. As I sacrifice, give me faith, help me to believe that you can and will keep your promise to give me the desires of my heart. Lord, I affirm the truth in my head, that I will only ever find my life by loosing it for your sake. Now please apply that faith to my heart as well. Help me Lord. Help me. Amen

ENCOURAGEMENT

Loose your life for his sake. Obey him. Trust him. And you WILL find your life.

Notes

-Day 32-
Rest

SCRIPTURE

O LORD, my heart is not proud, nor my eyes haughty; nor do I involve myself in great matters, or in things too difficult for me. Surely I have composed and quieted my soul; like a weaned child rests against his mother, My soul is like a weaned child within me. O Israel, hope in the LORD from this time forth and forever.

Psalm 131:1-3

PRAYER

Lord, daunting tasks loom on the horizon of my future, tasks that I don't want, don't feel comfortable with, and am not very good at, but tasks I must do, nonetheless. I ask for your peace. I ask that you would take away that low-grade ache that hangs in the back of my heart. Free me from the anxiety these future tasks bring. Give me the singular focus of resting in you today, Lord. Take the complicated matters, those things too difficult for me, and cause them to fade to the background of my mind... so that I can simply rest in your arms. Just like a mother's arms hold a calm and satisfied child, draw me to your soothing embrace, and rock my soul into a place of rest. And as I relax in your loving care, I pray that hope would spring forth and refresh me indeed. Amen.

ENCOURAGEMENT

Stop the flurry of anxious thoughts. Compose your heart. Quiet your mind. Sit with him and rest calmly in his love. Put ALL of your hope in him. He will not let you down.

Notes

-Day 33-
His Understanding and Power

SCRIPTURE

How great is our Lord! His power is absolute!
　His understanding is beyond comprehension!
The Lord supports the humble...

　　　　　　　　　　　　　Psalm 147: 5-6a

...Jesus said to them, "With people this is impossible, but with God all things are possible."

　　　　　　　　　　　　　Matthew 19:26

Now faith is the assurance of things hoped for, the conviction of things not seen.

　　　　　　　　　　　　　Hebrews 11:1

PRAYER

Lord, when life does not make sense, and what I long for seems impossible, it is good to remember your incomprehensible understanding and absolute power. You understand everything about my life and heart. You know. You have it figured out. You understand why. You know when. You could explain the details of how. And you see the what, before it ever comes to be. If I could only see what you see, I would rest. But then, that is the whole idea of building my faith Lord, so that I am convinced of those things I do not see, and am assured of that for which I hope. Give me faith, Lord. As I feel that my dreams are simply impossible, show me your power. Remind me, by something special today, that you are indeed God, and your power is absolute. You can do anything; anything. I pray that you would convince me that you could even do that one thing that I think is impossible. Convince my heart Lord. And as I humble myself in dependence upon your understanding and power, I ask that I would feel your hand encourage my spirit with your support. Amen.

ENCOURAGEMENT

God can do it. No barrier is too high for him, no situation too complicated, no dream beyond hope. Believe. Hope. And never give up.

Notes

-Day 34-
Renewal

SCRIPTURE

17 Unless the Lord had helped me, I would soon have settled in the silence of the grave.
18 I cried out, "I am slipping!" but your unfailing love, O Lord, supported me.
19 When doubts filled my mind, your comfort gave me renewed hope and cheer.

Psalm 94:17-19

PRAYER

Lord, help me please. There are times when the hurt is so deep, and the confusion so profound that all I can do is cry, "Help!" I don't know what I need and I don't know what to ask you to do. All I know is that I ache, and it feels as though my soul is settling down into the silence of the grave. I am slipping, Lord, but even now, at this moment I feel your love; a strong and unfailing love; a supportive love. Stability replaces slipping, and I feel safer. The doubts about your hand in my life, your ability to work good from bad, and your attentive love begin to dissolve as you simply flow comfort into my heart. It's a funny thing Lord, how the ache and the comfort can reside together there. But as the comfort comes, hope begins to grow again, and even a measure of joy. Thank you Lord. Thank you that somehow between the beginning of this prayer and the end you have given me a measure of renewal in my soul. I asked for help, and you gave it. Thank you Lord, thank you. Amen.

ENCOURAGEMENT

Cry out to him. Cry out when you don't know what to cry. He has unfailing love, comfort, hope and cheer. And he delights in renewing us. Just keep crying out. It will come.

Notes

-Day 35-
A Lift

SCRIPTURE

The Lord helps the fallen
   and lifts those bent beneath their loads.
                                          Psalm 145:14

PRAYER

Lord I have failed you at times, and need your help. Please help me today. It seems my mistakes follow me, the consequences of my past screams out in the most important parts of my life, creating more pain than it seems I can bear. I know that I am forgiven, but the residue of my shortcoming is always with me. The raw pain seems to be getting more intense, and I am beginning to bend beneath the load. Lift me Lord. Make me know the strength of your hand bearing the load so that I am no longer bent beneath it. Lift my spirit, heart and soul. Give me relief from the pain that follows me. Encourage me to know that your help is near, and your support is certain. Ease the weight now, Lord. Please. Amen.

ENCOURAGEMENT

He is near. He will help with the weight of your burden. He sees your bent and burdened soul, and is here to lift you. Take his help... it is the only certain help there is.

Notes

-Day 36-
His Presence

SCRIPTURE

7 I can never escape from your Spirit!
  I can never get away from your presence!
8 If I go up to heaven, you are there;
  if I go down to the grave, you are there.
9 If I ride the wings of the morning,
  if I dwell by the farthest oceans,
10 even there your hand will guide me,
  and your strength will support me.
11 I could ask the darkness to hide me
  and the light around me to become night—
  12 but even in darkness I cannot hide from you.
  To you the night shines as bright as day.
  Darkness and light are the same to you.
                                    Psalm 139:7-12

PRAYER

I am never alone, Lord. I am never alone. Even if I try to escape, I cannot. Even when I am by myself, I am not alone. This heavy feeling of aloneness is not reality, but is an illusion. I have your presence. Your Spirit resides with me. You are everywhere I could go, and you walk with me through every part of my journey. And although at times I think I would rather have someone with skin, indeed I am beginning to see that people with skin come and go, but you are constant. People fail, but you remain consistent. People will wander off, but you are a steady companion. People ignore, while you number the hairs of my head. People sometimes do not listen, or understand, or empathize, but you lavish your undivided attention, and your understanding of my deep heart. You enter my pain and sit with me there. You get me. And as I purposefully sit with you, alone, and engage your reality in this place, I begin to feel your wise guidance and strong support come to me. I begin to see that the spiritual truth of your presence is more real than a person with skin could ever be. And I begin to rest in that reality. I still miss the closeness of the touch of a kindred spirit, I still long for that soul connection, but the longing is different now. It is now an added grace to supplement the main course of a deeply intimate soul-connection with you. The more I learn to savor your presence, the more deeply will I be able to one day relish the gift of a person with skin who is fully engaged in listening, learning, and loving me. Thank you Lord, for your presence, and the guidance and support you bring. I need you. Amen.

ENCOURAGEMENT

Seek and savor the reality of his presence. Feel the depth of his lovingkindness. Value his guidance. Rest yourself on his support. And maybe one day, you will have someone with skin too. Never give up.

Notes

-Day 37-
His Provision

SCRIPTURE

I know how to live on almost nothing or with everything. I have learned the secret of living in every situation, whether it is with a full stomach or empty, with plenty or little. For I can do everything through Christ, who gives me strength.
Philippians 4:12-13

And this same God who takes care of me will supply all your needs from his glorious riches, which have been given to us in Christ Jesus.
Philippians 4:19

PRAYER

Lord, at different times, life has brought me both abundance and want. I have known fullness and need... and not just with regard to material things. I have felt the richness of love and the heartache of loss. I have known the fullness of friendship and the vacuum of loneliness. I have enjoyed the sunshine of gracious saints, and the darkness of the Pharisees' condemnation. I have felt the heights of joy and the depths of despair. Yes, my heart has known both a song and silence. And yet, through it all, you have been present; your strength has been available, and your glorious riches have met my every need. And so Lord, I ask that you would do that again today. Pour over me a wash of contentment this moment. Give me the strength to face my present day with confidence, a confidence that comes from having you at my side. Whisper in my ear Lord, "We can do this together, we can do this, stay with me, don't give up, keep walking with me." And then Lord, I ask that you would do something special for me... lavish a gift today that reminds me that you are meeting my every need, body, mind and soul. Surprise me with your grace and melt the remnants of doubt away Lord. Amen.

ENCOURAGEMENT

Relax in his provision. Rest in his strength. Find the joy in your present day and be content therein. Your gratitude will attract his blessings.

Notes

-Day 38-
Friends

SCRIPTURE

A friend loves at all times, and a brother is born for adversity.
Proverbs 17:17 (NASB)

PRAYER

Lord, it is during times of adversity that a friend is proven to be a true friend. Thank you for blessing me with people who care for me, even in the hard times. Thank you for those who are sensitive, and reach out with active love. Especially thanks for those who know my failures, and reach out still, for those who look past my mistakes to see my true heart. And Lord, I ask that you would bless those who show themselves to be friends indeed. As you pour forth your supporting love and comfort through them, I ask that a generous measure of that love and support would stick with them as well. Lord, bless them for blessing me, I pray. Amen.

ENCOURAGEMENT

Appreciate your friends, and be a friend indeed. And remember that when the going gets tough, true friendship shines.

Notes

-Day 39-
The Great Giver

SCRIPTURE

"Keep on asking, and you will receive what you ask for. Keep on seeking, and you will find. Keep on knocking, and the door will be opened to you. For everyone who asks, receives. Everyone who seeks, finds. And to everyone who knocks, the door will be opened.
"You parents—if your children ask for a loaf of bread, do you give them a stone instead? Or if they ask for a fish, do you give them a snake? Of course not! So if you sinful people know how to give good gifts to your children, how much more will your heavenly Father give good gifts to those who ask him.
                                            Matthew 7:7-11

PRAYER

Lord, you are indeed the great giver of gifts. You are the one to whom I plead. And you answer me by giving good gifts. I pray today that you would build my faith. I ask that you would move my heart to ask, seek and knock. Lord, I pray that I would be so intent on receiving the gifts you have, that I would not stop asking and seeking. I pray that the door that seems so tightly shut would open tomorrow because of my persistent knocking today. Revive my passion to plead Lord. Awaken my faith to believe that you are indeed a gracious heavenly Father, and that you love to give good gifts to your children. Do not allow me to settle for what I see today. Give me an assurance of things hoped for Lord. I pray that you would reach far into my heart and pull out the deepest longings, the longings so desperate that they hurt. I ask that you would light a fire of passion in my soul to ask until you answer, to seek until I find, and to keep on knocking until you open the door. And as I feel my weight on my knees, swell the hope in my heart. Amen.

ENCOURAGEMENT

Our Lord is sitting on the edge of heaven, waiting to lavish his blessed gifts. Ask him. Ask. And don't stop until he opens the door.

Notes

-Day 40-
Forgiveness and Obedience

SCRIPTURE

3 Lord, if you kept a record of our sins,
   who, O Lord, could ever survive?
4 But you offer forgiveness,
   that we might learn to fear you.

Psalm 130:3-4

"Blessed are those who mourn, for they shall be comforted.

Matthew 5:4 (NASB)

PRAYER
Lord, there is something in knowing what I deserve. The forgiveness that you have lavished draws me to respect you more. I pray that I would feel your forgiveness wash over me Lord. I ask that the full understanding of my failures would not pull me down, but would rather enrich my understanding of your forgiveness. Overwhelm me with the relief of that forgiveness. And Lord, as I come to know the richness of your grace, grow my passion for obedience. I pray that I would have a deep respect for you, and the obedience that you require. I ask that this wash of forgiveness would lead me to learn reverent obedience. Change my perspective, shape my passions, and soften my will because of a deeper awareness of your grace and your love. I pray that the grace you give will lead me to repentance where needed. And Lord, replace the mourning for my sin with the comfort of your forgiveness. Amen.

ENCOURAGEMENT

Your forgiveness comes at great cost to our Lord Jesus. His love for you moved him to be your substitute. Feel the depth of his love for you, and give that love back in your obedience. He wants all of you.

Notes

-Day 41-
Thy Word

SCRIPTURE

Your word is a lamp to guide my feet
    and a light for my path.

Psalm 119:105

PRAYER

Lord, when the complications of life begin to swirl around me, and the fog of my own heart drifts in, and bitter wind of other people's opinions whips up, I feel confused. I begin to doubt. I grope through the darkness, and wonder where the path is, and what obstacles might be in my future. I know *you* know, Lord, but I also long to know. It is in those moments of groping that I pray you would draw me to your word, Lord. I ask that I would linger long in your word, and not just the surface truth. I pray that I would ponder, dig, meditate, and explore your word for myself. Never allow me to settle for the status quo just because it is the standard line. Press me Lord, to study your word and make it my own. Sift my decisions, perspectives and actions through the truth of your word, and light my path Lord. I pray that illumination would be the order of the day, and that you would light the path before me, today, next week, and in the months and years to come. Amen.

ENCOURAGEMENT

His word has everything you need. Feast on it and follow the path it lights. And remember, it's God's word, so you need not be concerned about what everyone else thinks, just what he thinks. Walk the path he lights before you, in obedience and faith.

Notes

-Day 42-
Love Your Neighbor

SCRIPTURE

30 In reply Jesus said: "A man was going down from Jerusalem to Jericho, when he fell into the hands of robbers. They stripped him of his clothes, beat him and went away, leaving him half dead.
31 A priest happened to be going down the same road, and when he saw the man, he passed by on the other side.
32 So too, a Levite, when he came to the place and saw him, passed by on the other side.
33 But a Samaritan, as he traveled, came where the man was; and when he saw him, he took pity on him.
34 He went to him and bandaged his wounds, pouring on oil and wine. Then he put the man on his own donkey, took him to an inn and took care of him.
35 The next day he took out two silver coins and gave them to the innkeeper. 'Look after him,' he said, 'and when I return, I will reimburse you for any extra expense you may have.'
36 "Which of these three do you think was a neighbor to the man who fell into the hands of robbers?"
37 The expert in the law replied, "The one who had mercy on him." Jesus told him, "Go and do likewise."

Luke 10:30-37 (NIV)

PRAYER

Lord, there are times when I am in need of a true neighbor. There are seasons when my spirit feels beaten, stripped, and abandoned. I find myself wounded, confused, and unable to help myself. I am simply in need. Thank you so much Lord, for those

Samaritans who have looked closely enough to see the desperateness. Lord, thank you that there are some who have listened long enough to understand the wounds and feel a depth of compassion for me. And thank you that their compassion was active enough to sooth and bandage the wounds, even at the sacrifice of time and energy. Lord, thank you that I was not required to meet a certain religious qualification for help, but that help just flowed from the love of a neighbor. I am grateful to you Lord for these honorable saints who are fulfilling the great commandment to love their neighbor. May they feel your pleasure for the wounds they have bandaged. And may I pass that same active compassion to others who hurt... even to those who may have passed me by in my need; even to those Lord. Amen.

ENCOURAGEMENT

It only takes one Samaritan to effect a great healing in your soul. Receive that gift, and go and do the same. Learn from those who passed you by, and love them like they should have loved you.

Notes

-Day 43-
A Generous Wisdom

SCRIPTURE

Dear brothers and sisters, when troubles come your way, consider it an opportunity for great joy. For you know that when your faith is tested, your endurance has a chance to grow. So let it grow, for when your endurance is fully developed, you will be perfect and complete, needing nothing. If you need wisdom, ask our generous God, and he will give it to you. He will not resent your asking.

James 1:2-5

PRAYER

Lord, it is when troubles persist that I am in special need of wisdom. Knowing your truth is easier than the wisdom of applying your truth to the complexities of life. I pray that you would create in me a sense of need and longing for your wisdom. There will be times when new horizons present to me, when big decisions loom over me, when perception and insight beyond my ability are required. As those times come, Lord, I pray that you would swell in my heart an instinct to ask you to unleash your generous supply of wisdom. I pray that your wisdom would make my decisions insightful, my timing perfect, and my intuition divine. But most of all Lord, I pray that my faith in your present wisdom would put my heart at peace. No matter how alone I may be Lord, make me know beyond a shadow of a doubt that you are present to guide me with the warmth of your wisdom. And may that warmth melt my fear away, and give birth to joy. Do that for me this week Lord. Amen.

ENCOURAGEMENT

It is when you feel most alone, and most overwhelmed that God's generous supply of wisdom will be most appreciated. He will pull through for you this week as you ask. He is never far, and always listening for your plea.

Notes

-Day 44-
Be Blessed

SCRIPTURE

So it came about, when Joseph reached his brothers, that they stripped Joseph of his tunic, the varicolored tunic that was on him; and they took him and threw him into the pit...

Then some Midianite traders passed by, so they pulled him up and lifted Joseph out of the pit, and sold him to the Ishmaelites for twenty shekels of silver. Thus they brought Joseph into Egypt...

The LORD was with Joseph, so he became a successful man. And he was in the house of his master, the Egyptian. Now his master saw that the LORD was with him and how the LORD caused all that he did to prosper in his hand. So Joseph found favor in his sight and became his personal servant; and he made him overseer over his house, and all that he owned he put in his charge. It came about that from the time he made him overseer in his house and over all that he owned, the LORD blessed the Egyptian's house on account of Joseph; thus the LORD'S blessing was upon all that he owned, in the house and in the field.
                        Genesis 37:23-24, 28; 39:2-5 (NASB)

PRAYER

Lord, I ask that your presence and its accompanying blessing would be with me in the same way it was with Joseph. Joseph found himself far from home, adjusting to a new place, new people, and a new life. And it all came about because of the impact of the sin of others. But you honored Joseph's loyalty and obedience to you, and added something special to everything he did. I ask you Lord, to bless me in all I do, all I touch. Lift my heart so that I see the good in all that comes my way, so that I see your hand of blessing in it all. As the events of life seem to slide across the table and drop into my lap, I pray that you would give me the grace to see each event as it comes, to field it, and to respond to it with honor and dignity. And may those events actually be transformed into magnificent blessings, just as they were in Joseph's life. When life gets harder, and when I feel as though I have been forgotten and abandoned in a jail in Egypt, I ask that even there your hand of blessing would rest upon me and cause my heart and all I touch to flourish. Cause me to find favor in the sight of those around me. Bless me Lord, bless me indeed. Amen

ENCOURAGEMENT

Alone is never truly alone. He is with you, and his blessing is all round you. Watch it come, and receive it as from him. He loves you. He loves you indeed.

Notes

-Day 45-
Pray Big

SCRIPTURE

The effective prayer of a righteous man can accomplish much. Elijah was a man with a nature like ours, and he prayed earnestly that it would not rain, and it did not rain on the earth for three years and six months. Then he prayed again, and the sky poured rain and the earth produced its fruit.

James 5:16b-18 (NASB)

PRAYER

Lord, help me to pray big. I confess that my small faith would have me make excuses for unanswered prayer before I even pray. The inertia of my heart believes that because I am not extraordinary, I must pray small. Lord, remind me of the importance of faith. Remind me of the Elijahs... ordinary people who accomplished the extraordinary through earnest prayer. Refresh my awareness of the critical importance of personal righteousness to the equation of effective prayer. And Lord, move me to pray great feats of prayer. Release me to ask for the absurd. Free my heart to reach for the sky, and believe that you are big enough and gracious enough to answer me. Make me aware of what I might miss because of cowardly prayers. Make me an ordinary person like Elijah, who dares to ask for the extraordinary, and believes that you will answer. And change the course of my life because of it. Amen.

ENCOURAGEMENT

Cleanse your hands, roll up the sleeves of your faith, and ask big. He longs to respond to your bold faith. He already knows the deep desires of your heart. And he is waiting to respond to your pleas. Be extraordinarily normal... like Elijah.

Notes

-Day 46-
Your Mind and His Peace

SCRIPTURE

Don't worry about anything; instead, pray about everything. Tell God what you need, and thank him for all he has done. Then you will experience God's peace, which exceeds anything we can understand. His peace will guard your hearts and minds as you live in Christ Jesus.

And now, dear brothers and sisters, one final thing. Fix your thoughts on what is true, and honorable, and right, and pure, and lovely, and admirable. Think about things that are excellent and worthy of praise. Keep putting into practice all you learned and received from me—everything you heard from me and saw me doing. Then the God of peace will be with you.

Philippians 4:6-9

PRAYER

O Lord, peace of heart is one of your great inventions, one of your most wonderful gifts. Were it not for your peace, I would be left to the agitation of mind and fear of heart that comes from not knowing the future. What an ache of anxiety I feel at times, Lord. I see through the fog of my mind futures that will never be, and feel in my heart today the pain of tomorrow that may never come. And deep down I know the waste of emotion. Lord, I ask that you would take my thoughts captive, and fix my mind on those things that will lift me out of the dungeon of fear and into the light of hope. Train my mind Lord, to dwell on the quality of this life you have given. Saturate me with your focus. And somewhere in this renewed perspective I ask that you would bring a peace that is so calming that I wonder at it.

Deep within I pray that I would feel the calm of a mountain lake on a still morning. And when I look fixedly on this calm, may I see the towering mountains of your love reflected there. May I know today, in a fresh way, the power of a renewed mind to bring your peace. And when I look at tomorrow, may I see the beauty of the good gifts you are yet to give me. Amen.

ENCOURAGEMENT

Think hard on everything that God is. Allow those dark elements of this world to be a blurred backdrop, only adding to the beauty of God's gifts. Fix your thoughts on that beauty, and not only will you have the peace of God, but the presence of the God of peace as well.

Notes

-Day 47-
A Cry for Mercy

SCRIPTURE

Jesus was approaching Jericho, a blind man was sitting by the road begging... And he called out, saying, "Jesus, Son of David, have mercy on me!"

Those who led the way were sternly telling him to be quiet; but he kept crying out all the more, "Son of David, have mercy on me!"

And Jesus stopped and commanded that he be brought to Him; and when he came near, He questioned him, "What do you want Me to do for you?"

And he said, "Lord, I want to regain my sight!" And Jesus said to him, "Receive your sight; your faith has made you well."

Immediately he regained his sight and began following Him, glorifying God; and when all the people saw it, they gave praise to God.
Luke 18:35, 38-43 (NASB)

PRAYER

Lord, I have a hurt in my life that has surrounded me for so long that survival has demanded I adjust. It is a pain that I cannot fix, that limits my wholeness, and dulls hope on the horizon of my future. I need a touch from you in either my heart, or my circumstance, or both. I pray that I would feel your presence close by. I cry out for your mercy. Though others may not understand or approve of my plea, yet I cry out all the more fervently Lord. And when you respond to my heart, may I be ready to articulate simply and precisely what

I want you to do for me. May that desire so burn in my heart that there is no pause in my response. May I tell you what I want, with a heart that brims with belief. And Lord, I pray that you would see my faith, and grant my heart's desire. Heal my hurt Lord. Fulfill my longing. Make my dream come true. And Lord, in so doing, may you enjoy the sweet aroma of my undying gratitude and praise. Amen.

ENCOURAGEMENT

Mercy. It flows from his heart to yours. It is released by the cry of faith. Cry out for his Mercy, and keep crying out.

Notes

-Day 48-
Unfailing Love

SCRIPTURE

7 Come quickly, Lord, and answer me,
    for my depression deepens.
  Don't turn away from me,
    or I will die.
8 Let me hear of your unfailing love each morning,
    for I am trusting you.
  Show me where to walk,
    for I give myself to you.
9 Rescue me from my enemies, Lord;
    I run to you to hide me.
10 Teach me to do your will,
    for you are my God.
  May your gracious Spirit lead me forward
    on a firm footing.

                                  Psalm 143:7-10

PRAYER

Lord, there are moments in my life, when heaviness of heart would surely drown me in a sea of circumstance, were it not for you. I know in those moments that your help, your presence, and your unfailing love are necessary for my very survival. Dear God, I ask that this morning you would land your unfailing love upon the awareness of my heart. May that love melt helplessness and hopelessness into a deep pool of trust. Guide me, Lord, with your love. Show me precisely where to take my next step. And after I take that step, show me the next. I give myself completely to you Lord, to walk just as you would have me to walk. Rescue me from danger. Teach me your will. Lead me. As I ponder your present love, I feel the safety of hiding in your care.

Give me both a firm footing and a forward movement as your spirit leads. Help me Lord, help me. Amen

ENCOURAGEMENT

Watch for his unfailing love this day. It will come to you in unexpected ways. Receive it. Relish it. And walk in it.

Notes

-Day 49-
Incomprehensible Love

SCRIPTURE

"And I pray that you may have power, together with all the saints, to grasp how wide and long and high and deep is the love of Christ, and to know this love that surpasses knowledge."
Ephesians 3.18

PRAYER

Lord, there are some days that I long for the love of a person. I want to be cared for. I want to be important and needed. I want to be listened to, understood, and admired. I want to capture the attention and affection of someone important to me. But Lord, when I look deep within, I know that the love I really need is yours. I begin to see how amazing your love for me really is. I begin to see that the breadth of your love covers all, the length of your love is never-ending, the height of your love is immeasurable, and the depth of your love reaches the most important parts of my being. And as I begin to see this love more clearly, my heart is touched and my life is changed. Be my best friend today, Lord. Amen.

ENCOURAGEMENT

Always remember, the one who loves you most matters most... our Lord himself. Soak it in, bask in it, and allow that love to change you. It will never let you down; never.

Notes

-Day 50-
Pour Out Your Troubles

SCRIPTURE

1 I cry out to the Lord;
   I plead for the Lord's mercy.
2 I pour out my complaints before him
   and tell him all my troubles.
3 When I am overwhelmed,
   you alone know the way I should turn.
                                   Psalm 142:1-3

PRAYER

Lord, I just have a need to come before you and unburden my heart. I feel the pain of trouble in my life, and the pressure gives vent to a respectful complaint. I have a case to build for what I would like you to do. I pray that you would release the constraints on my heart, and allow me the freedom to tell you what I will. Lord, bid me follow the Psalmist example, and cry out with a plea for your mercy and a detailing of all my troubles. Somewhere in the expression there is hope and comfort to be found, I know. So pull from my heart the depth of pain that I hold there. I pray that I would release that pain into your hands, with details. You are big enough to handle even the raw blast of emotion I feel. You are able to sift through the words and hear my true heart. I have no risk of being misunderstood by you Lord. Give me permission in my soul to speak from that place of being overwhelmed. And as I do, I ask that you would reassure me that you alone understand the situation, and you alone know the change in direction that I need. From the expression of pain, show me your direction Lord. Make it as clear as the day. Help the eyes of my heart to see it. Help the feet of my will to follow your direction Lord, follow it completely. Amen.

ENCOURAGEMENT

There is no shame in feeling pain, and in venting the full blast of your emotions to God. He can handle it. Tell him where you hurt, why you want it to change, and what you want him to do. It's called prayer, and it may not look like a church prayer, but it will certainly look like a prayer of Psalm 142. God will be pleased, and you might just find some direction waiting at the other end.

Notes

-Day 51-
A Sure Help

SCRIPTURE

4 I look for someone to come and help me,
    but no one gives me a passing thought!
  No one will help me;
    no one cares a bit what happens to me.
5 Then I pray to you, O Lord.
    I say, "You are my place of refuge.
    You are all I really want in life.
6 Hear my cry,
    for I am very low.
  Rescue me from my persecutors,
    for they are too strong for me.
7 Bring my soul out of prison
    so I can thank you.

                              Psalm 142:4-7a

PRAYER

It is an empty feeling to be abandoned in my most desperate time of need, Lord. And yet, it is when I feel the sting of consequences for my own mistakes that I am most likely to be ignored by those who were my friends. I hope for someone to help me, but they put me out of their minds. No one seems to care, Lord. And the very ones who could add comfort, multiply pain by their neglect. Yet, it is in these times that I am pressed to turn to you Lord. Move my heart to find my shelter in you. I ask that I would see you as the only one who could ever really fill that empty place in my life. I ask that you would hear my cry, lift my spirit, and rescue me from those who would spill their judgements upon me. Their accusations are too strong for me to handle Lord. Please release my soul from this prison of judgmental eyes. Free me to live again. Bring me home Lord, so that I can lavish my thanks upon you. Amen.

ENCOURAGEMENT

Seek God's attentive and caring help most. It is the only sure help there is.

Notes

-Day 52-
Get and Give Mercy

SCRIPTURE

Then Jesus told this story to some who had great confidence in their own righteousness and scorned everyone else: "Two men went to the Temple to pray. One was a Pharisee, and the other was a despised tax collector. The Pharisee stood by himself and prayed this prayer: 'I thank you, God, that I am not a sinner like everyone else. For I don't cheat, I don't sin, and I don't commit adultery. I'm certainly not like that tax collector! I fast twice a week, and I give you a tenth of my income.'

"But the tax collector stood at a distance and dared not even lift his eyes to heaven as he prayed. Instead, he beat his chest in sorrow, saying, 'O God, be merciful to me, for I am a sinner.' I tell you, this sinner, not the Pharisee, returned home justified before God. For those who exalt themselves will be humbled, and those who humble themselves will be exalted."

Luke 18:9-14

PRAYER

Lord, cultivate in me that posture of heart that sees in one view both my sin and your mercy. Keep me from confidence in my own righteousness and the unseemliness of scorn that comes with it. This confidence comes so subtly Lord, almost unaware. It seeps in over years of religiosity and overtakes that once humble heart. And we forget from whence we came. And we think that we made our own righteousness. And we so easily look down from our self-made loftiness. Guard my heart from that place Lord. Give me that beautiful balance of awareness of my own sin, and yet trust in your mercy for forgiveness and cleansing. Make me feel the unworthiness and sorrow of my sin, and yet the justification that comes to me though your mercy. And Lord, may you somehow create a genuine humility in me. Amen.

ENCOURAGEMENT

Ok, so you have sinned. Feel your sorrow fully, and cry for his mercy. He will be pleased with your humility of heart, and will declare you righteous. Then go, and give what you have been given, mercy rather than judgment.

Notes

-Day 53-
Draw Near

SCRIPTURE

As Jesus and the disciples continued on their way to Jerusalem, they came to a certain village where a woman named Martha welcomed him into her home. Her sister, Mary, sat at the Lord's feet, listening to what he taught. But Martha was distracted by the big dinner she was preparing. She came to Jesus and said, "Lord, doesn't it seem unfair to you that my sister just sits here while I do all the work? Tell her to come and help me."
But the Lord said to her, "My dear Martha, you are worried and upset over all these details! There is only one thing worth being concerned about. Mary has discovered it, and it will not be taken away from her."
Luke 10:38-42

Draw near to God and He will draw near to you.
James 4:8a

For I know the plans I have for you," declares the LORD, "plans to prosper you and not to harm you, plans to give you hope and a future.
Jeremiah 29:11 (NIV)

PRAYER

Dear Lord, there resides beneath the surface of my heart a dull ache regarding my future. What will my life become? Will my needs ever be met? Will my longings be fulfilled? Is there hope? Will my worries become realities? Will my fears take flesh? Which will come true, my nightmares or my dreams? Lord, I do all that I can do, all that you call me to do, but there is so much that is outside of my control. I confess that at times I feel both helpless and hopeless. Help me Lord. Help me to seek you with more of my heart. Give me that singular focus that draws me to long for your attention and yearn for your nearness. I cry out to you Lord, please listen. Please listen, and please reveal yourself to me. Give me that same comfort that you gave your people, give me a comfort to know that you have plans for good, not disaster; that I do indeed have a hopeful future Lord. I need comfort. I ask you to enter that place of ache deep inside, and dissolve it into peaceful trust in you and your grace. Help my faith. Amen.

ENCOURAGEMENT

God knows the plans he has for you. He knows. Draw near to him. Enjoy him. Rest in him. Trust him.

Notes

-Day 54-
His Grace

SCRIPTURE

He who gives an answer before he hears, it is folly and shame to him.
Proverbs 18:13 (NASB)

Do not judge so that you will not be judged.
Matthew 7:1 (NASB)

For the whole Law is fulfilled in one word, in the statement "YOU SHALL LOVE YOUR NEIGHBOR AS YOURSELF." But if you bite and devour one another, take care that you are not consumed by one another.
Galatians 5:14-15 (NASB)

[Of the woman caught in adultery and brought before Jesus to be stoned]
Jesus straightened up, and said to them, "He who is without sin among you, let him be the first to throw a stone at her."
John 8:7 (NASB)

PRAYER

Lord, there are times when the hateful eyes of Pharisees are upon me, and the venom of their condemning words threatens to bite and devour me. They feel qualified to judge, although they know nothing of the facts, have not walked my road, and cannot see my deep heart. They relish an opportunity to hurl a stone. Lord, protect my heart and soul from these. Cause me to turn toward your grace, receiving your forgiveness, and continuing to walk in repentance and renewed obedience. Help me to know and feel your favor and grace on my life. Guard me from their bite, and make the accusations roll off my heart like water off a duck's back. And I ask that the beautiful grace that you have given me, I would extend patiently and kindly to my accusers, that they may come to their senses and stop throwing stones. Amen.

ENCOURAGEMENT

Hear our Lord's voice clearly through the crowd of your accusers, "Neither do I condemn you, go and sin no more." (John 8:11)

Notes

-Day 55-
As Unto the Lord

SCRIPTURE

1   "Beware of practicing your righteousness before men to be noticed by them; otherwise you have no reward with your Father who is in heaven.
2   "So when you give to the poor, do not sound a trumpet before you, as the hypocrites do in the synagogues and in the streets, so that they may be honored by men. Truly I say to you, they have their reward in full.
3   "But when you give to the poor, do not let your left hand know what your right hand is doing,
4   so that your giving will be in secret; and your Father who sees what is done in secret will reward you.
5   "When you pray, you are not to be like the hypocrites; for they love to stand and pray in the synagogues and on the street corners so that they may be seen by men. Truly I say to you, they have their reward in full.
6   "But you, when you pray, go into your inner room, close your door and pray to your Father who is in secret, and your Father who sees what is done in secret will reward you.
Matthew 6:1-6 (NASB)

Whatever you do, do your work heartily, as for the Lord rather than for men, knowing that from the Lord you will receive the reward of the inheritance. It is the Lord Christ whom you serve.
Colossians 3:23-24

PRAYER

Lord, there is much in my life that goes unnoticed by people. There are ordinary everyday tasks that I do to serve others that feel unseen or taken for granted by many. The time I spend in prayer, the energy I put into meditation on your truth, and my honest self-reflection goes unseen by any other person on this planet. I grow in my faith, in the peace I feel from you, in the depth of obedience in my heart, and no one sees that but you. Ah, but Lord, YOU see it. I ask that you would make me more aware of your watchful eye upon the good I do. Help me to know that you log my good deeds, and will reward them richly one day. May I feel your smile upon my life, Lord. May I feel the satisfaction of having your pleasure. And as I come to appreciate more the fullness of your smile, may my every motive be refined. May all that I do, big and small, be done as unto you Lord. Amen.

ENCOURAGEMENT

God sees those acts of service that go unnoticed, and he is aware of the good things in your heart. He sees, and he will reward you. Be encouraged, and please don't give up. We need you.

Notes

-Day 56-
God our Father

SCRIPTURE

Grace to you and peace from God our Father and the Lord Jesus Christ.

Romans 1:7b

PRAYER

Lord, you have given me an earthly father who loved me dearly. Although not perfect, he has gifted me with a treasure of memories, lessons, and love that will last forever. And most of all, he has taught me something of you, my Heavenly Father. I pray that today you would bring to my heart the good gifts I have received from my earthly father, and would thus be moved with gratitude toward you, my Heavenly Father. I pray that as I reflect on my Dad, that I would have a moment of insight that would give me a deeper understanding of you Lord. As I remember his embrace, may I receive yours. As I reflect on his wisdom, may I ponder yours. As I feel his love, may I savor yours. And as I feel my Dad's smile, fill me with your grace and your peace. Amen.

ENCOURAGEMENT

Earthly fathers may come and go, but your Heavenly Father is always with you; always; right beside you; through anything. He will never leave you; never.

Notes

-Day 57-
The Wings of Eagles

SCRIPTURE

27 O Jacob, how can you say the Lord does not see your troubles?
   O Israel, how can you say God ignores your rights?
28 Have you never heard?
   Have you never understood?
   The Lord is the everlasting God, the Creator of all the earth.
   He never grows weak or weary.
   No one can measure the depths of his understanding.
29 He gives power to the weak and strength to the powerless.
30 Even youths will become weak and tired, and young men will fall in exhaustion.
31 But those who wait on the Lord will find new strength.
   They will soar high on wings like eagles.
   They will run and not grow weary.
   They will walk and not faint.

Isaiah 40:27-31

PRAYER

Lord, the more I wait, the more it seems that you do not see my troubles. And some seasons of life are so unfair that it feels as though you are ignoring me entirely. Those seasons of emptiness and aloneness are consuming, almost like a low-grade terror that builds in the background of my heart and threatens to overwhelm me. In those seasons Lord, I pray that you would remind me of who you are; the everlasting God, Creator of all the earth. Bring to my heart a vision of the amazing strength, endurance, and understanding that you make available to me. Lord, quiet my heart.

Still me. Move me into your presence just to sit in silence, and wait; wait, Lord. Remove from my mind the fear of the unknown, the worry of the future, the pain of the present. Give my heart a singular focus Lord... YOU. Open a conduit from your heart to mine. And as I wait, pour forth upon my spirit a generous supply of strength to overcome my fears, of understanding to see my future, and of endurance to face my present. Lift me high above my circumstances as my wings catch the wind of your spirit. Make my spirit soar Lord. Give me that surge of strength, that depth of endurance I need to walk my path. And when this comes to me Lord, may it be sudden and supernatural. May I know for sure that it comes from you. May I see WAITING as the conduit that carries this strength. And Lord, because of that, may the word WAIT become sweet to my soul indeed. Amen.

ENCOURAGEMENT

Make the waiting count. Wait long, not for your hopes and dreams, but wait on your Lord. Sit in his presence often and long. Worship him as creator and sustainer. Delight yourself in the intimacy of his presence. And feel yourself soar.

Notes

-Day 58-
The Great Healer

SCRIPTURE

2   Be gracious to me, O LORD, for I am pining away; heal me, O LORD, for my bones are dismayed.
3   And my soul is greatly dismayed; but you, O LORD-- how long?
4   Return, O LORD, rescue my soul; save me because of your lovingkindness.

Psalm 6:2-4

30   And large crowds came to Him [Jesus], bringing with them those who were lame, crippled, blind, mute, and many others, and they laid them down at His feet; and He healed them.

Matthew 15:30

PRAYER

You, O Lord, are the one who heals. Though sin takes its toll, both mine and others', yet you heal Lord. I ask that this day you would give me a quiet reassurance that your power is able, and your grace is sufficient, to heal even a greatly dismayed soul. Give me faith Lord. I come to you now, pining away and yet searching for your healing. I ask that you would flood my heart with a healing balm that could only come from the divine. I feel that you are reaching into my heart, and touching me in ways that are beyond counseling, beyond self-help, and beyond understanding. May I feel your touch Lord. And as I do, I ask that I would perceive healing. Don't just bandaged my wounds, Lord, but take the cancer of soul away. Reach my deep places, my confused places, my blocked places, my fearful places. Heal me... completely... unmistakably... and soon, I pray. Amen.

ENCOURAGEMENT

He came to heal. Be dismayed, that's ok. Ask how long, he understands. But plead with him to give you the healing that your heart and soul needs today. Ask him. He is the great healer.

Notes

-Day 59-
Calming the Storm

SCRIPTURE

23 When He got into the boat, His disciples followed Him.
24 And behold, there arose a great storm on the sea, so that the boat was being covered with the waves; but Jesus Himself was asleep.
25 And they came to Him and woke Him, saying, "Save us Lord; we are perishing!
26 He said to them, "Why are you afraid, you men of little faith?" Then He got up and rebuked the winds and the sea, and it became perfectly calm.
27 The men were amazed, and said, "What kind of a man is this, that even the winds and the sea obey Him?"

Matthew 8:23-27

PRAYER

Lord, today I can feel the storms around my life overwhelming me with swells of pain and sorrow. The hurt I carry feels as deep as the ocean that brings the storm. The confusion around me bites like a bitter wind in my face. And some days I feel like I am going under for the last time. I feel as if the boat of my life is becoming swamped. I ask at this moment Lord, that you would rebuke the circumstances of my life, and calm the storm around me. Bring calm and peace to my heart. Amaze me as you amazed the men on the boat. Draw me to worship you in amazement as I see what you have done in my life. And through it Lord, I pray that you would build my faith. Amen.

ENCOURAGEMENT

He sees the storm, and yet he is calm. His strength can calm the storm around you. Ask him. And then trust him.

Notes

-Day 60-
Bless the Children

SCRIPTURE

15 One day some parents brought their little children to Jesus so he could touch and bless them. But when the disciples saw this, they scolded the parents for bothering him.
16 Then Jesus called for the children and said to the disciples, "Let the children come to me. Don't stop them! For the Kingdom of God belongs to those who are like these children. 17 I tell you the truth, anyone who doesn't receive the Kingdom of God like a child will never enter it."

Luke 18: 15-17

PRAYER

Lord, you have placed some young people around my life that I might impact them for your kingdom. You give me opportunities to bless these young lives in wonderful ways. Today I pray that you would indeed bless them through me, both through my example and my words. Swell my heart with the satisfaction of knowing that you have touched a tender soul through me. Help me to know that your touch in their lives is eternal and powerful. And as you give me a glimpse of the fruit of your work in their lives, encourage me I pray. Amen.

ENCOURAGEMENT

The difference you are making in these children's lives is eternal, and will bring an eternal reward. Hang in there.

Notes

-Day 61-
Strength and Encouragement

SCRIPTURE

As soon as I pray, you answer me;
you encourage me by giving me the strength I need.
                                                    Psalm 138:3

PRAYER

I cry out to you Lord. Answer me quickly. Please make your answer carry with it your strength. I feel weak today, Lord. It feels like the circumstances of my life require more than I have to give. I am not sure that I can go on, but there seems to be no escape. My heart feels the heaviness of discouragement. Oh Lord, I ask that you would give a double portion of your strength to me this moment. And as that strength lands in my heart, I pray that it would bear the fruit of encouragement. Lift my spirits. Fill me with hope. Cover me with peace. May that strength give me the confidence I need to walk the path before me, with honor and grace. Amen.

ENCOURAGEMENT

It may be that the answer to your prayer comes, not as the answer you expected, but as the answer you needed... strength. Be encouraged... you are just that important to him.

Notes

-Day 62-
Acts of Kindness

SCRIPTURE

34 "Then the King will say to those on his right, 'Come, you who are blessed by my Father; take your inheritance, the kingdom prepared for you since the creation of the world.
35 For I was hungry and you gave me something to eat, I was thirsty and you gave me something to drink, I was a stranger and you invited me in,
36 I needed clothes and you clothed me, I was sick and you looked after me, I was in prison and you came to visit me.'
37 "Then the righteous will answer him, 'Lord, when did we see you hungry and feed you, or thirsty and give you something to drink?
38 When did we see you a stranger and invite you in, or needing clothes and clothe you?
39 When did we see you sick or in prison and go to visit you?'
40 "The King will reply, 'I tell you the truth, whatever you did for one of the least of these brothers of mine, you did for me.'
Matthew 25:34-40 (NIV)

PRAYER

Lord, needs abound, in both those around me, and in me. There are not only the physical needs, but also emotional hurts that run deep. Souls are hungry, thirsty, alone, uncared for, sick, and imprisoned. They need a touch from you Lord, a touch that you have designed to come through us, and a touch that is sometimes neglected by those who can give it. I pray two things Lord. First, I pray that you would prompt my heart to extend kindness to those persons you put in my heart this week. Meet their needs through me Lord. I pray that you would touch the deep places of their hearts through me. And equally, I ask that you would bring to me a few who will act as your instruments of care toward me. I pray that you would prompt their hearts to extend acts of kindness to me in just the way I need, in just the manner that is best, and at just the perfect time. And as you do, I pray that you would close a circle of community, a circle that has you at the center. Amen.

ENCOURAGEMENT

When you reach out and meet a need, it has the same impact and the same reward as if you did it for our Lord himself. Keep your awareness keen, and watch our Lord bring a perfect opportunity to touch "him" this week.

Notes

-Day 63-
Living in Harmony

SCRIPTURE

1 How wonderful and pleasant it is when brothers live together in harmony!
2 For harmony is as precious as the anointing oil that was poured over Aaron's head, that ran down his beard and onto the border of his robe.
3 Harmony is as refreshing as the dew from Mount Hermon that falls on the mountains of Zion. And there the Lord has pronounced his blessing, even life everlasting.

Psalm 133:1-3

PRAYER

Lord, give us harmony I pray. There is too much hate, too much fermented anger, and too many nurtured grudges. The embers of misunderstandings are fueled into raging fire, and the sting of pain is returned seven fold. Lord, I ask that you would make me aware this week of my part in the dissonance around my web of relationships. Search my heart and show me how to be harmonious, and with whom that should start. Move me to do my part in being at peace with those around me, even those who show hate to me. Restore friendships. Resolve conflict. Reunite families. Replenish love. Move me to show the love to others that you have first shown to me. And may we all experience the beauty, satisfaction, and refreshment of harmony among us Lord. Amen.

ENCOURAGEMENT

Forgive an offense. Touch a need. Understand a deep heart. Be a friend. And feel the refreshment of harmony.

Notes

-Day 64-
His Abundance

SCRIPTURE

7 How precious is your unfailing love, O God!
   All humanity finds shelter
      in the shadow of your wings.
8 You feed them from the abundance of your own house,
      letting them drink from your river of delights.
9 For you are the fountain of life,
      the light by which we see.

Psalm 36:7-9

PRAYER

Life is in you, Lord. Shelter from the storms of life is found in you. Abundance and delight come from you. Lord, today I purpose to bask in the generous gifts you have given me. I pray that I would feel alive indeed, and would know that this life comes to me from you. I see your abundance in my life and heart. I would stay very near you, seeking shelter from the difficulties of life. Allow me to drink from your river of delights and feel the satisfaction of soul that comes. Lord, lavish upon me your precious and unfailing love. And may my heart be overcome with gratitude because of it. Amen.

ENCOURAGEMENT

His love will never fail. His shelter is secure and sure. His abundance feeds, and his delights quench the thirst of your soul. Stay close to him, and live indeed.

Notes

-Day 65-
Live Close to Him

SCRIPTURE

4 The one thing I ask of the Lord— the thing I seek most— is to live in the house of the Lord all the days of my life, delighting in the Lord's perfections and meditating in his Temple.
5 For he will conceal me there when troubles come; he will hide me in his sanctuary. He will place me out of reach on a high rock.
6 Then I will hold my head high above my enemies who surround me.

Psalm 27:4-6

PRAYER

Lord, I pray that you would put within my heart a passionate desire to live my life in a continual place of connectedness with you, as if I were living in your house. I pray that I would think deeply upon your perfections, your attributes, and your beauty. And as I see you, may my heart leap with delight, as seeing my best friend and the object of my deepest affections. May I long for closeness with you Lord. And I pray that when those moments of inevitable trouble come, you would hide me in that place of closeness with you, protecting me from the harm my enemies would seek. May I feel so loved and cared for by you, that I can hold my head high as a valued son of the King. Amen.

ENCOURAGEMENT

The place of secure protection in times of trouble is to be near our Lord. Live close to our Lord as the dwelling place of your soul, and delight your heart in his beauty. He will never let you down.

Notes

-Day 66-
Embrace His Love

SCRIPTURE

35 Who shall separate us from the love of Christ? Shall trouble or hardship or persecution or famine or nakedness or danger or sword?
36 As it is written: "For your sake we face death all day long; we are considered as sheep to be slaughtered."
37 No, in all these things we are more than conquerors through him who loved us.
38 For I am convinced that neither death nor life, neither angels nor demons, neither the present nor the future, nor any powers,
39 neither height nor depth, nor anything else in all creation, will be able to separate us from the love of God that is in Christ Jesus our Lord.

Romans 8:35-39 (NIV)

PRAYER

Lord, I pray that you would reach into the tender parts of my heart and make me know your lavish love. The part of my heart that is broken, I pray your love would heal. The part of my heart that is desperate, I pray your love would comfort. The part of my heart that longs, I pray your love would fill. And the part of my heart that hurts, I pray your love would sooth. Lord, I need you, I need to know that I am important to you and loved by you. I need to know that your love will never fail me, no matter what trouble swirls around in my life. I need to know that your love makes life worth living Lord. Fill me with your love today I ask. Amen.

ENCOURAGEMENT

He loves you. When all others fail you, He will not. Embrace his love in the midst of your pain. It is sweet and sure.

Notes

-Day 67-
Feast Upon His Word

SCRIPTURE

During that time the devil came and said to him, "If you are the Son of God, tell these stones to become loaves of bread."
But Jesus told him, "No! The Scriptures say,
'People do not live by bread alone, but by every word that comes from the mouth of God.
Matthew 4:3-4

How sweet your words taste to me;
  they are sweeter than honey.
Psalm 119:103

PRAYER

Lord, I pray that you would nourish my soul with the sweetness of your word. I ask that when the temptations come to divert my focus to the temporal, you would feed me with the eternal. I pray that when I am pulled to worry about my needs, you would give me what I truly need. Strengthen me with truth as it flows from your heart to mine Lord. Make my mind simmer on that truth, pondering its application to my life. Bring to my remembrance the bread of truth you have given my soul in days past, and nourish me again as you press this truth into my everyday. And Lord, I pray that as I taste the sweetness of your word, my soul would be satisfied. May I live indeed, by every word that comes from you to me. Amen.

ENCOURAGEMENT

His words to you are words of true love. Dine upon them. Savor them. Feast generously. They are food for your soul.

Notes

-Day 68-
Rebuilding

SCRIPTURE

Praise the Lord!
How good to sing praises to our God!
How delightful and how fitting!
2 The Lord is rebuilding Jerusalem
and bringing the exiles back to Israel.
3 He heals the brokenhearted
and bandages their wounds.
4 He counts the stars
and calls them all by name.
5 How great is our Lord! His power is absolute!
His understanding is beyond comprehension!
6 The Lord supports the humble,
but he brings the wicked down into the dust.
Psalm 147:1-6

PRAYER

Lord, it brings such hope to know that you are the rebuilder. You rebuild broken hearts, broken worlds, broken spirits and broken dreams. I pray that you would show me the power of your attentive care. Bandage my wounds, and begin the healing. Display your power in the reconstruction of my life. May your understanding so penetrate my life that I feel known, understood, accepted and loved by you. And as the load of life begins to bend my back, may your support be powerful and sweet. May my hope rest completely in you, Lord. Amen.

ENCOURAGEMENT

He calls the stars by name, and yet you are more brilliant and more important still. He knows and understands you. He heals. He has both the power and the understanding to do whatever it takes to re-build you. Trust him today, and walk closely with him into tomorrow.

Notes

-Day 69-
Unfair Criticism

SCRIPTURE

13 Who is there to harm you if you prove zealous for what is good?
14 But even if you should suffer for the sake of righteousness, you are blessed. AND DO NOT FEAR THEIR INTIMIDATION, AND DO NOT BE TROUBLED,
15 but sanctify Christ as Lord in your hearts, always being ready to make a defense to everyone who asks you to give an account for the hope that is in you, yet with gentleness and reverence;
16 and keep a good conscience so that in the thing in which you are slandered, those who revile your good behavior in Christ will be put to shame.
17 For it is better, if God should will it so, that you suffer for doing what is right rather than for doing what is wrong.

1 Peter 3:13-17 (NASB)

PRAYER

Lord, today I feel the harshness and accusation of a critical crowd. Help me to find hidden in the refuse of their words those small nuggets of truth you have for me. Help me to discern when their words are merely the judgments of small people who prefer the delicacies of slander to truth. Make me patient when assumptions prevail over honest inquiry. Give me grace when they squint from a distance, choosing the facts they prefer, but never seeking a clear view of the whole. Season my responses when they purport to know the intentions of my heart, without ever hearing. And help me to forgive when they cloak their judgments with religiosity. Lord, thank you for opening my heart to your promptings, for moving me to confess, repent and obey. And in that, I ask that you would help me to feel the cleanness of a good conscience before you. I pray that you would remove from me any fear of their intimidation. Calm my heart so that I may rest in your smile upon me. And Lord, as I continue to walk closely to you, I pray that you would reveal the shame of my accusers. Amen.

ENCOURAGEMENT

Your Lord knows you. He sees right down to your very soul, and understands your heart. Don't allow these small people to steal your peace or direct your paths. Walk with our Lord, and follow your deep heart.

Notes

-Day 70-
God's Protection from Enemies

SCRIPTURE

7 Though I am surrounded by troubles, you will protect me from the anger of my enemies. You reach out your hand, and the power of your right hand saves me. 8 The LORD will work out his plans for my life— for your faithful love, O LORD, endures forever. Don't abandon me, for you made me.

Psalm 138:7-8

PRAYER

I am surrounded by troubles some days Lord. My enemies seem to sense when I am low, and under the pretense of seeking to understand, their anger lashes out with accusation. I feel unheard, misunderstood, and judged. They know well what to say, and how to strike. I sometimes feel in need of a Samaritan who will render emotional care and healing. Yet there is none, Lord, but you. Thank you that the power of your right hand reaches out and saves me. Thank you that you will work out your plans for my life with a faithful love. And most of all, thank you that you will never abandon me. I rest in your strong arms. Amen.

ENCOURAGEMENT

Hear well the promptings of our Lord, yet deafen your ear to the anger of your enemies. If they spoke the words of God, they would also emulate their Lord's faithful love. Though many may abandon you, our Lord will be ever with you.

Notes

-Day 71-
Our Prayers, God's Miracles

SCRIPTURE

Then Elijah said to Ahab, "Go get something to eat and drink, for I hear a mighty rainstorm coming!"
So Ahab went to eat and drink. But Elijah climbed to the top of Mount Carmel and bowed low to the ground and prayed with his face between his knees.
Then he said to his servant, "Go and look out toward the sea."
The servant went and looked, then returned to Elijah and said, "I didn't see anything."
Seven times Elijah told him to go and look.
Finally the seventh time, his servant told him, "I saw a little cloud about the size of a man's hand rising from the sea."...And soon the sky was black with clouds. A heavy wind brought a terrific rainstorm...

        1 Kings 16:41- 45 (selected)

The earnest prayer of a righteous person has great power and produces wonderful results. 17 Elijah was as human as we are, and yet when he prayed earnestly that no rain would fall, none fell for three and a half years! 18 Then, when he prayed again, the sky sent down rain and the earth began to yield its crops.

        James 5: 16-18

PRAYER

Lord, I have many things in my heart for which I pray, actions I would like you to take, situations I would like you to influence, hopes and dreams for my tomorrow, longings for today, desires on other's behalf. I have need of strength, faith, hope, love, peace, and joy. I would have you effect growth in me and others. So Lord, I ask that you would make my prayers earnest. May I pray with a depth of passion that moves the angels to take wing and deliver my requests to you in haste. I ask that you would clothe me with the righteousness of Jesus so that my prayers come to you in power and produce results. Make me to fall down before you in humility and dependence, pleading my heart day and night. And Lord, I ask that you would hear my prayers, and answer them in your grace. As I delight myself in you, may you grant me the desires of my heart for which I plead. Amen.

ENCOURAGEMENT

Elijah was no different that you. Allow your prayers to flow from a deep earnestness and powerful righteousness. Then stand back and watch God work miracles indeed.

Notes

-Day 72-
Weeping ... then Joy

SCRIPTURE

For his anger lasts only a moment, but his favor lasts a lifetime!
Weeping may last through the night, but joy comes with the morning.

Psalm 30:5

PRAYER

Lord, there are days when I weep, if not with outward tears, then with inward sorrow of soul. I feel the heaviness of heart that comes from my mistakes, from the pain I have caused, and from the effect of other's sin. There is no escape from this pain. There is no road around it, only a hard path through it. The dark clouds of painful emotions hover above, and the pelting rain of circumstance is relentless. The stinging winds of consequence buffet me about without mercy, and for a moment I know your anger Lord, but only for a moment. For though the darkening storm lasts through what seems to be a long night, yet the sunshine of joy is on the horizon. Pain is but for a season, and then you bring joy. And the sunshine of joy is sweeter for having endured the storm of pain. The flower of your favor is more beautiful because of the rain you allow. So Lord, please take me through this night as weeping overwhelms me. Hold me. Help me. Comfort me. And in faith, I long for the morning you will wipe my tears away, and give me joy. Amen.

ENCOURAGEMENT

Hold on through the night. The morning will be better. Trust him for that.

Notes

-Day 73-
Compassion

SCRIPTURE

11 You, O LORD, will not withhold your compassion from me; your lovingkindness and your truth will continually preserve me.

17 Since I am afflicted and needy, let the Lord be mindful of me. You are my help and my deliverer; do not delay, O my God.
Psalm 40:11,17 (NASB)

PRAYER

Lord, I am afflicted and needy. I ask that you would help me to know that's ok. Some of my pain is due to things beyond my control, and some is because of my own sin. But regardless Lord, I need compassion, both from your people and from you. I ask that you would move in the hearts of those around me to show compassion. I pray that you would give them a deep awareness and understanding of my pain. Help them to look beyond the veneer of "togetherness" and see the true hurt. Help them to crawl out of their own world long enough to sit alongside me and feel the depth of my pain with me. Move them to show compassion for me, actively, purposefully, and often. And Lord, even in those seasons when your people fail me, hold me close to yourself, and make me know that you truly do understand everything, and that you feel my pain with me. May I know the sweetness of your compassion. Amen.

ENCOURAGEMENT

His compassion is real, powerful, and sweet. Own it. And remember, you are worthy of the compassion of his people. Their abandonment speaks more of their character than your worthiness. Forgive them, and lean on our Lord.

Notes

-Day 74-
Quiet Confidence

SCRIPTURE

18   This is how the birth of Jesus Christ came about: His mother Mary was pledged to be married to Joseph, but before they came together, she was found to be with child through the Holy Spirit.
19   Because Joseph her husband was a righteous man and did not want to expose her to public disgrace, he had in mind to divorce her quietly.
20   But after he had considered this, an angel of the Lord appeared to him in a dream and said, "Joseph son of David, do not be afraid to take Mary home as your wife, because what is conceived in her is from the Holy Spirit.
21   She will give birth to a son, and you are to give him the name Jesus, because he will save his people from their sins."
22   All this took place to fulfill what the Lord had said through the prophet:
23   "The virgin will be with child and will give birth to a son, and they will call him Immanuel"-- which means, "God with us."

Matthew 1: 18-25 (NIV)

PRAYER

Lord, Joseph heard you, believed you, and followed you regardless of the whispers of well-meaning people in the shadows. I pray that you would give me the same ear to hear your direction, the same faith to walk your path, and the same quiet confidence to disarm the impact of other's opinions. Amen.

ENCOURAGEMENT

Don't live your life based on the popular opinion of others. Is your heart right before God, and your conscience clear? Then walk the path he has put before you. It does not matter how right they think they are. It only matters what God tells your heart.

Notes

-Day 75-
The Shepherd's Care

SCRIPTURE

The LORD is my shepherd;
I have all that I need.

Psalm 23:1

PRAYER

You are my shepherd Lord. You love me deeply. You know my pain. You understand, when those around me could not possibly. You see every empty place, every heartache, every moment of aloneness, every fear, and the despair that sometimes envelops it all. You are my shepherd. You know the real needs that even I do not comprehend. As I come to know your shepherd care, I feel your tenderness and strength flow together in a way that answers my cries and meets my needs. The pain remains, and my aching soul still throbs, but it's different knowing your care; more secure, more at peace. I ask that at this moment you would fill my heart with a quiet reminder of your shepherd care. May I feel your presence, your protection, and your healing. And may I be overwhelmed with the knowing that all my needs are met in you. Amen.

ENCOURAGEMENT

The great shepherd offers you all that you truly need. Rest in his care. Rest.

Notes

-Day 76-
The Love of a Father

SCRIPTURE

8 The Lord is compassionate and merciful, slow to get angry and filled with unfailing love.
9 He will not constantly accuse us, nor remain angry forever.
10 He does not punish us for all our sins;
he does not deal harshly with us, as we deserve.
11 For his unfailing love toward those who fear him is as great as the height of the heavens above the earth.
12 He has removed our sins as far from us as the east is from the west.
13 The Lord is like a father to his children, tender and compassionate to those who fear him.
14 For he knows how weak we are;
he remembers we are only dust.
         Psalm 103:8-14

PRAYER

Lord, there are few things that inspire as much wonder and awe as the vastness of the heavens you created. And yet that endless expanse of height is a picture of something far more powerful and precious to me, your unfailing love for me. That love moves you to mercy. You forgive me. You have thrown my sins as far away as the east is from the west. You are my tender and compassionate father. Lord, you know my weaknesses, every one, and yet love me still. I pray that you would come to me with this strong and tender love, and fill me up to overflowing. As I gaze into the sky on a clear night, may I feel overwhelmed by the vastness of your love. And may I feel with sureness that your love is indeed unfailing, no matter what. Amen.

ENCOURAGEMENT

No matter whose love may come and go from your life, our Lord's love will never fail. Never. Lean on his unfailing love.

Notes

-Day 77-
A Humble Heart

SCRIPTURE

"So humble yourselves under the mighty power of God, and at the right time he will lift you up in honor."
1 Peter 5:6

PRAYER

Lord, I ask that you would keep my heart soft and easily molded by your hand. I pray that I would not be occupied with the need to be honored by people, but that I would long for your approval and smile. I pray that a humble spirit would so groom the substance of my heart that when the heat of adversity comes, it would soften my heart like wax rather than harden it like clay. May that softness take away some of the pain of your work, and give you an open space to work in my life. And I pray that as others see the clear marks of your shaping hand, that I would receive honor from you at just the right time. Amen.

ENCOURAGEMENT

Concentrate on cultivating a genuine humility in your own heart. Leave the honoring to God. He will work his miracles in his own time.

Notes

-Day 78-
Nourishing the Soul

SCRIPTURE

"People are like grass; their beauty is like a flower in the field. The grass withers and the flower fades. But the word of the Lord remains forever."... So get rid of all evil behavior, deceit, hypocrisy, jealousy, and all unkind speech. Like newborn babies, crave the pure spiritual milk of the word so that you will grow into a full experience of salvation. Cry out for this nourishment, now that you have had a taste of the Lord's kindness.

1 Peter 1:24, 2:2-3

PRAYER

Oh Lord, my heart has felt the violence of imperfect people, and the loss of those I love. Coping with this pain sometimes drains my reserves, and leaves me weak and spent. Please feed me with your words of life. Well up within me a longing for the milk of your word. Lead me to those passages of scripture that will strengthen and sustain my spirit. Make those words sweet to my taste and nourishing to my soul. I know well that people fade from my life like flowers of the field, so Lord, make me know equally well that your words of life will never fail me. Make me to lean upon you. At this moment Lord, I ask that you would reach my deepest places with the sweet sustenance of your truth. Amen.

ENCOURAGEMENT

Feast upon his eternal words. Savor the taste, and texture of his truth. It will nourish you, and never fail you.

Notes

-Day 79-
Calming the Emotional Storm

SCRIPTURE

Watch over your heart with all diligence, for from it flow the springs of life.
                                         Proverbs 4:23 (NASB)

And do not be conformed to this world, but be transformed by the renewing of your mind, so that you may prove what the will of God is, that which is good and acceptable and perfect.
                                         Romans 12:2 (NASB)

PRAYER

Lord, there are times when my mind throbs with a constant pounding of unwelcome thoughts about past events, present concerns, and an uncertain future. It is as though my thoughts feed an emotional swirl of regret, anxiety, and worry. The emotions trigger more thoughts, which feed more emotions until the swirl has become a downward and darkening spiral. I pray that at this moment you would set me free Lord. Transform my thoughts. Renew my mind. Refocus the lens of my mind onto those good and beautiful gifts you have given. Allow me to bask in your forgiveness and healing from yesterday, your strength and wisdom for today, and the hope of my desires and dreams for tomorrow. Cause my heart to swell with gratitude for the love I feel from you, the faith you are building in me, and the bright hope you have put on my horizon. May I feel the storm within me calm, and the sun of your grace begin to warm my soul. And tonight may I fall into a peaceful sleep, secure in your strong arms. Amen.

ENCOURAGEMENT

Rest your weary mind on his love, and grace, and forgiveness, and compassion, and wisdom, and strength, and hope. Rest your thoughts, and watch your emotions follow. You are his. He is always near.

Notes

-Day 80-
Groan Your Desires to God

SCRIPTURE

In the same way the Spirit also helps our weakness; for we do not know how to pray as we should, but the Spirit Himself intercedes for us with groanings too deep for words... He intercedes for the saints according to the will of God. And we know that God causes all things to work together for good to those who love God, to those who are called according to His purpose.

Romans 8:26-28 (selected NASB)

PRAYER

Lord, I find myself in such a place of pain and confusion that I am not even sure how to pray. My soul aches for both your will and my heart's desire. Swirling around the mix is a healthy dose of people's sinful actions and the attendant consequences that flow. Making sense of it all, and articulating a prayer that is in line with your will, and will work good from the chaos just seems beyond me. Thank you that even now, your Spirit takes my deep heart and conveys it accurately in a prayer that is according to your will. Thank you that you will take everything in my life and work it together for my good. I ask that you would help me to feel your Spirit groaning with me, pushing together in a direction that will ultimately work your perfect purpose and plan from the imperfection that surrounds my life. Hear my desire for your will Lord, and honor that with an answer that makes my heart leap. Amen.

ENCOURAGEMENT

He knows your heart and his. He can do this, he can work the magic of good from even this. Groan your desires to God through His Spirit, and watch him weave the sovereign tapestry for your good and his glory.

Notes

-Day 81-
Peaceable Wisdom

SCRIPTURE

But the wisdom from above is first pure, then peaceable, gentle, reasonable, full of mercy and good fruits, unwavering, without hypocrisy. And the seed whose fruit is righteousness is sown in peace by those who make peace.

James 3:17-18

If possible, so far as it depends on you, be at peace with all men... Do not be overcome by evil, but overcome evil with good.

Romans 12:18, 21 (NASB)

PRAYER

Lord, there are some who hover around my life who are simply not peaceable. The sting of their judgment penetrates like a biting wind. And although they offer accusations with a religious cloak, they are far from gentle or merciful. The fruit of the seeds of their words are far from peaceful and much closer to the evil accusations of the enemy. I pray that in spite of this, you would keep my heart in peace today Lord. I ask that you would help me to release ownership of their words, judgments, and responses, and embrace my own heart and actions only. May I do those things that make for peace, whether or not they are accepted. May you protect me from the evil judgments around me, and move me to simply do what is right, from my heart. And Lord, I ask that as I step forward with courage and do what I know pleases you, that I would overcome the evil judgments with the good of your grace. I ask that you would surround me with your peace today Lord. Amen.

ENCOURAGEMENT

Stand up, march forward and do good. Do good no matter what anyone else says. Do it with courage. Do it in the face of accusations, misunderstanding, and judgments. Overcome their evil with your good. And rest in his peace.

Notes

-Day 82-
Love Him

SCRIPTURE

One of them, an expert in religious law, tried to trap him with this question: "Teacher, which is the most important commandment in the law of Moses?"
Jesus replied, "'You must love the Lord your God with all your heart, all your soul, and all your mind.' This is the first and greatest commandment. A second is equally important: 'Love your neighbor as yourself.' The entire law and all the demands of the prophets are based on these two commandments."

Matthew 22:35-40

PRAYER

Lord, when the complications of life swirl around me, and my mind spins with questions and the anxiety of tomorrow's wonderings, I pray that you would slow me down and bring me back to the simple truths of loving you and loving others. Lord, well up within my heart a deepening love for you. Take every ounce of passion, every joule of energy, every synapse of my mind and make them pulsate with a love for you. Cultivate in me a sense of worshipping you in every moment of my day. And as I sense this love for you washing over my every activity, thought and feeling, may your peace overwhelm and envelop my very soul. In that peace, may I spill your love into the lives of those I touch. May the love I give come back to me a hundred fold. Amen.

ENCOURAGEMENT

Love well. Make him the center of your love, and people the overflow. And watch to see if God will not measure back to you more love that you could have ever imagined. Watch and see.

Notes

-Day 83-
The Promised Land

SCRIPTURE

8 "Therefore, be careful to obey every command I am giving you today, so you may have strength to go in and take over the land you are about to enter. 9 If you obey, you will enjoy a long life in the land the Lord swore to give to your ancestors and to you, their descendants—a land flowing with milk and honey! 10 For the land you are about to enter and take over is not like the land of Egypt from which you came, where you planted your seed and made irrigation ditches with your foot as in a vegetable garden. 11 Rather, the land you will soon take over is a land of hills and valleys with plenty of rain—12 a land that the Lord your God cares for. He watches over it through each season of the year!

Deuteronomy 11:8-12

PRAYER

Lord, deep in my heart I long for a promised land in my life. Circumstances and events have brought hardship, and am in a season of life that is much more like Egypt, where everything seems to come by labor and toil. I pray that you would give me the hope of a promised land on the horizon of my future. I ask that you would cause the sun to rise on a new season of my life soon. Make me aware that you are beginning to take me there, even now. And Lord, in preparation for that day, draw me closer to you, deepen my love for you, and make me obedient to you in every area of my life. I ask that this commitment to you will give me the strength needed to enter this wonderful place in my life. Give me the faith to believe that you will slay every giant that stands between me and that Promised Land. Amen.

ENCOURAGEMENT

Trust him. Obey him. And when the moment arrives, step forward in faith. He will give you the strength you need to enter this land of his gracious provision.

Notes

-Day 84-
A Friend

SCRIPTURE

A real friend sticks closer than a brother.
Proverbs 18:24b

Encourage the fainthearted, help the weak, be patient with everyone.
1Thessalonians 5:14b (NASB)

PRAYER

Lord, I know what it is to be fainthearted and weak. The load of emotions I am under sometimes seems unbearable. My heart faints and the knees of my soul are weak. And yet, there seems to be no one who sticks closer than a brother. No one calls. No one encourages. No one helps. It feels as though no one cares. And rather than the pain being lessened by a brother, the absence of a friend makes the pain greater still. Lord, it ought not be so. I pray that you would rouse the hearts of your people to remember what it is to show active love to one in need. I pray that they would see beyond their busyness and see the shadow of those sitting alone in pain. Cause their excuses to be consumed like wood, hay and straw Lord. Help them to remember what it was like to be loved by you when they were unable to love back. Bring to their heart the times they were the ones in need, helplessly hoping for a Samaritan to come along and bandage their wounds. Move them to initiate actions of care and compassion and love Lord. Move me to do the same. Move us now, I pray. Amen.

ENCOURAGEMENT

Be the friend you long to have. Give of your heart what you can and when you can. And wait for God to give you a friend indeed.

Notes

-Day 85-
Pour out the Pain

SCRIPTURE

41 And He [Jesus] withdrew from them about a stone's throw, and He knelt down and began to pray,
42 saying, "Father, if You are willing, remove this cup from Me; yet not My will, but Yours be done."
43 Now an angel from heaven appeared to Him, strengthening Him.
44 And being in agony He was praying very fervently; and His sweat became like drops of blood, falling down upon the ground.
                        Luke 22:41-44 (NASB)

PRAYER

Lord, as my heart feels the agony of my current lot, I ask that you would move me to pray my heart with great fervor. Turn my agony into pleadings. Give me freedom to bring my requests to you unashamedly, and yet melt my will into yours Lord. May I feel my agony, release my pain, and submit my will. And as I am in the midst of that agony Lord, I ask that you would bring an angel from heaven to my side to strengthen me so that I might walk the road you have set before me with dignity and grace. Amen.

ENCOURAGEMENT

It's ok to feel your pain and pour out your agony in prayer. It's ok.

———————————

Notes

-Day 86-
Hope Indeed

SCRIPTURE

Blessed be the God and Father of our Lord Jesus Christ, who according to His great mercy has caused us to be born again to a living hope through the resurrection of Jesus Christ from the dead,
1 Peter 1:3 (NASB)

3 And not only this, but we also exult in our tribulations, knowing that tribulation brings about perseverance;
4 and perseverance, proven character; and proven character, hope;
5 and hope does not disappoint, because the love of God has been poured out within our hearts through the Holy Spirit who was given to us.
Romans 5:3-5 (NASB)

24 For in hope we have been saved, but hope that is seen is not hope; for who hopes for what he already sees?
25 But if we hope for what we do not see, with perseverance we wait eagerly for it.
Romans 8:24-25 (NASB)

PRAYER

Lord Jesus, thank you that your resurrection gives me great hope for forgiveness from the past, power for the present, and heaven in the future. Thank you that the resurrection speaks of new life, new hope, and new beginnings. I pray that you would bring hope to my heart. I have experienced a storm of tribulation this past year, and I pray that this tribulation has built the stamina of perseverance, and that somehow it has shown the quality of my character. Now Lord, I ask that you would well up in my heart hope of every sort. Make me feel your complete forgiveness. Make me know your power to persevere in my present. Make me feel beautiful and powerful of heart and character. And give me the faith to feel the assurance of those hopes and dreams that linger in my heart. Give me the faith to feel a conviction that those things I have yet to see are indeed coming one day. Flood my whole person with an overwhelming sense of hope that washes away my doubts and fears forever. Amen.

ENCOURAGEMENT

Our Lord has seen your pain and your perseverance. As he rests his eyes on your proven character he affirms your heart indeed. Have faith, rest in hope, and bask in his undying love.

Notes

-Day 87-
Life and Peace

SCRIPTURE

For the mind set on the flesh is death, but the mind set on the Spirit is life and peace,
Romans 8:6 (NASB)

PRAYER

Life and peace Lord, is what I ask for my life at this moment. Move me to focus my mind on that which your Holy Spirit within me would bring. Push out those dismal ponderings of dark futures, and move me to dream of beautiful possibilities Lord. Break into my mind with light and paint hopeful futures. Make me know that you take even the dark events of my past and weave them into light. Help me to feel your forgiveness and love and confidence and smile. And Lord, as I am filled up to overflowing with the ponderings of your future blessings, please fill me with life and peace. Please flood my emotions with your peace as a result of filling my mind with your spirit. May my purposeful intentions be to digest in my mind only those brilliant and hopeful blessings that you have yet to give. Amen.

ENCOURAGEMENT

The thoughts you choose to meditate upon will have a profound effect upon your emotions. Choose to dwell on the hope of his lavish blessing. Choose.

Notes

-Day 88-
A Restored Soul

SCRIPTURE

He makes me lie down in green pastures; He leads me beside quiet waters. He restores my soul;
Psalm 23:2-3a (NASB)

PRAYER

I grow so weary some days Lord. I feel the depletion that comes from running a spiritual marathon. My soul is parched, and my heart exhausted. And some days I have no tears left to cry. Oh Lord, I pray that you would refresh me this moment. I pray that you would cause my soul to stretch out in a pasture that is cool, green and shady. As I rest there, feed me Lord. Give me those thoughts, those truths, those encouragements that my weary heart needs most. Revive me Lord. Give me cool waters to refresh me in a place free of anxiety, a place of peace. Renew me. Bring my soul back to a place of calm assurance and readiness. Repair my brokenness. Heal my wounds. Restore my soul I pray Lord. Amen

ENCOURAGEMENT

He is your Shepherd. He will give you green pastures and quiet waters. Savor them, and he will restore your soul. He will. Trust him.

Notes

-Day 89-
Just Like Heaven

SCRIPTURE

"Your kingdom come. Your will be done, on earth as it is in heaven."

Matthew 6:10 (NASB)

PRAYER

Oh God in heaven above, I ask that your Kingdom would come to my heart, and your will would be done in my life, as it is done in heaven. Flood my heart with a sense of being under your kingship, honoring you with my life, obeying you, seeking to be close to you. I ask that all of the best things that you would will for my life would come true. I ask that you would permeate me with your incomprehensible peace, pushing out of my heart any trace of anxiety or panic. I ask that you would give me a deep sense of inner joy, no matter my circumstances. I pray that hope would spring forth as a blossom. Give me a faith that is calmly assured of those things I hope for. And give me such a feeling of being loved that I just can't help but smile. Fill my heart with light and life Lord. Make me taste today, those perfect gifts that you will one day will into my life in heaven. Today Lord, give them to me today... Thy Kingdom come, Thy will be done in my life as it is in heaven. Amen.

ENCOURAGEMENT

The enemy of your soul has been rebuked. The God of heaven is coming to work his will in your heart and life. Yearn for it. Expect it. Savor it. Light and life is being prayed into you.

Notes

-Day 90-
His Closeness

SCRIPTURE

"... and lo, I am with you always, even to the end of the age."
Matthew 28:20b (NASB)

Surely goodness and lovingkindness will follow me all the days of my life, and I will dwell in the house of the LORD forever.
Psalm 23:6 (NASB)

PRAYER

Lord, I ask that from this moment onward, I would feel the comfort of your constant presence. Brush me often with the wings of those angels you have sent to minister your care and strength in my life, so that I never doubt your love and involvement. And as I sense your presence I ask that my fellowship with you would be a sweet taste to my soul from now and forever. Make me to know the depth of intimacy with you that few in this world have known Lord. Reveal yourself to me in very personal and powerful ways. Fill my soul with the richness that comes from dwelling with you Lord, not just seeing you occasionally, but living and abiding in your presence. Touch the deep place in me with you Lord God. May I never be the same because of it. Amen.

ENCOURAGEMENT

He is with you. He is, and always will be. Welcome him, enjoy him, long for him every moment. As you do, you will dwell in the house of the Lord now and forever.

Notes

Index

1 Corinthians 4: 1-4 50
1 Kings 16:41- 45 (selected) 158
1 Peter 1:24, 2:2-3 172
1 Peter 1:3 188
1 Peter 3:13-17 154
1 Peter 5:6 170
1 Thessalonians 5:14b 184

2 Chronicles 16:9 36
2 Corinthians 1:3-4 76

Abundance 144

Brokenhearted 20
Burdens 70

Closeness 196
Colossians 3:23-24 126
Comfort 56, 76
Compassion 162
Confidence 164
Courageous Faith 54
Criticism 154
Cry for Mercy 110

Delight 28
Despair 18
Deuteronomy 11:8-12 182
Direction 32
Discipline 24
Draw Near 122

Eagles 130
Enemies 156
Ephesians 3.18 114

Faith 64
Fears 26
Forgiven 22

Forgiveness	96
Friend	184
Friends	92
Galatians 5:14-15	124
Genesis 22:1-12	78
Genesis 37:23-24, 28; 39:2-5	104
Grace	124
Gratitude	72
Harmony	142
Healer	132
Heaven	194
Hebrews 11:1	18, 82
Hebrews 12:5-12	24
His Care	52
His Presence	88
His Provision	90
Hope	38, 188
Humble Heart	170
II Thessalonians 2:16-17	56
Incomprehensible Love	114
Isaiah 26:3	74
Isaiah 40:27-31	130
James 1:2-5	68, 102
James 3:17-18	178
James 4:8a	122
James 5: 16-18	158
James 5:16b-18	106
Jeremiah 29:11	38, 122
John 8:7	124
Joy	160
Kindness	140
Love	114
Love of a Father	168
Love Your Neighbor	100
Luke 10:30-37	100
Luke 10:33-37	70

Luke 10:38-42	122
Luke 18: 15-17	136
Luke 18: 1-8	34
Luke 18:35, 38-43	110
Luke 18:9-14	120
Luke 22:41-44	186
Mark 14: 35-36	34
Matthew 1: 18-25	164
Matthew 10:29-31	52
Matthew 11:28-30	66
Matthew 15:30	132
Matthew 19:26	82
Matthew 22:35-40	180
Matthew 25:34-40	140
Matthew 28:20b	196
Matthew 4:3-4	150
Matthew 5:4	76, 96
Matthew 6:10	194
Matthew 6:1-6	126
Matthew 6:28b-30	52
Matthew 7:1	70, 124
Matthew 7:7-11	94
Matthew 8:23-27	134
Mercy	120
Miracles	158
Numbers 13-14 (selected scriptures)	54
Obedience	78, 96
Pain	186
Peace	74
Peaceable	178
Persistent	34
Philippians 4:12-13	90
Philippians 4:19	90
Philippians 4:6-7	44
Philippians 4:6-9	108
Promised Land	182
Proverbs 17:17	92
Proverbs 18:13	124

Proverbs 18:24b ... 184
Proverbs 3:5-6 ... 58
Proverbs 4:23 ... 174
Psalm 103:8-14 ... 168
Psalm 119:103 ... 150
Psalm 119:105 ... 98
Psalm 130:3-4 ... 96
Psalm 131:1-3 ... 80
Psalm 133:1-3 ... 142
Psalm 138:3 ... 138
Psalm 138:7-8 ... 156
Psalm 139:1-6 ... 46
Psalm 139:7-12 ... 88
Psalm 142:1-3 ... 116
Psalm 142:4-7a ... 118
Psalm 143:7-10 ... 112
Psalm 145:14 ... 86
Psalm 147: 5-6a ... 82
Psalm 147:1-6 ... 152
Psalm 20:1-5 ... 30
Psalm 23:1 ... 166
Psalm 23:2-3a ... 192
Psalm 23:6 ... 196
Psalm 27:13-14 ... 18
Psalm 27:4-6 ... 146
Psalm 30:5 ... 160
Psalm 34:16-19 ... 20
Psalm 36:7-9 ... 144
Psalm 37:23-24 ... 32
Psalm 37:3-4 ... 28
Psalm 37:7 ... 40
Psalm 40:11,17 ... 162
Psalm 40:5 ... 38
Psalm 51 (selected verses) ... 22
Psalm 56:8 ... 52
Psalm 57:1 ... 60
Psalm 57:2-3 ... 62
Psalm 57:7-10 ... 64
Psalm 6:2-4 ... 132
Psalm 75:1 ... 72
Psalm 77: 1-3 ... 48
Psalm 94:17-19 ... 84

Purpose	62
Rebuilding	152
Renewal	84
Rest	66, 80
Restored Soul	192
Romans 1:7b	128
Romans 12:18, 21	178
Romans 12:2	174
Romans 5:3-5	188
Romans 8:24-25	188
Romans 8:26-28	176
Romans 8:28	42
Romans 8:35-39	148
Romans 8:6	190
Shelter	60
Shepherd's Care	166
Storm	134
Strengthening	36
Troubles	116
Trust	58
Understanding	82
Unfailing Love	112
Waiting	40
Weeping	160
Wisdom	102
Worries	44
Your Mind	108
Zephaniah 3:16	26

Order This Book

Order copies of this book directly from the publisher at:

davidaedwardsonline.com

Other Versions of this Book

<u>A Prayer for Him: Devotionals for the Hurting Heart</u> contains the same devotionals as this book, except the prayers are formed to be prayed for a man, with a blank appearing in place of a man's name, i.e.

> Lord, I ask that you would breathe faith into (_____'s) heart so that he knows beyond a shadow of a doubt that...

<u>A Prayer for Her: Devotionals for the Hurting Heart</u> contains the same devotionals as this book, except the prayers are formed to be prayed for a lady, with a blank appearing in place of a lady's name, i.e.

> Lord, I ask that you would breathe faith into (_____'s) heart so that she knows beyond a shadow of a doubt that...

Personalized versions of <u>A Prayer for Him</u> and <u>A Prayer for Her</u> are available, where a specific name appears:
- On the cover (i.e. "A Prayer for Jason"),
- In the dedication
- In each prayer

> Lord, I ask that you would breathe faith into *Jason's* heart so that he knows beyond a shadow of a doubt that...

Give the gift of personalized encouragement to someone you care about.

3949421

Made in the USA